Contents

Acknowledgements   vii

How to use this book   ix

1   Activities around songs, poetry and rhymes   1

2   Home corners and talk areas   15

3   Drama, role-play and mime   30

4   Story boxes, story bags and story telling   47

5   Debating and questioning   66

6   Pictures and picture books   78

7   Circle time and talk games   93

References and book list   107

Index   111

Acknowledgements

I would like to thank the following for their help in the making of this book:

The children of Greenleys First School with whom all these activities were carried out and who always do their best and rise to the occasion!

The staff of Greenleys First School, particularly Heather Stelling and Geraldine Fellows, for their ideas and continual support.

The Milton Keynes literacy consultants team for their interest and enthusiasm.

My family for putting up with less of my time and more of my irritability!

Special thanks to Christopher for 'doing' the dragon picture, and my husband Jean Pierre for his unstinting help with 'computer issues'!

I would also like to acknowledge and thank all the authors, illustrators, publishers, and organisations mentioned in this book. They have contributed indirectly over the years to my classroom practice and in doing so have helped me deliver lessons that I believe have inspired and motivated many children.

How to use this book

The aim of this book is to provide a practical guide to activities that require children to use language in a variety of situations. It is by providing lots of opportunities for speaking and listening that children, hopefully, can develop and extend their language skills.

The QCA 1999 *Guidance for Teaching Speaking and Listening Skills in Key Stages 1 and 2* mentions, in the Introduction, the importance of children's ability to speak and listen to their language development and learning in school. It goes on to say, 'Most children come into school with some ability to hold a conversation, persuade, argue and entertain others. School provides new contexts for talk that demand new and greater oral skills.'

If children have not yet developed the vocabulary or had the life experiences that will help them to access the language used in school, learning will be a challenge. Most of us have experienced situations where children have not known the meaning of a word that we took for granted they would know, such as the Year 3 teacher who found not one child in her class could define what a hedge was.

By being aware of this and providing opportunities for children to use and develop their language skills it is possible for teachers and other practitioners to make a real difference to children's learning. Children's attainment can be raised through speaking and listening activities and lessons that incorporate speaking and listening. This in turn can help to raise self-esteem and confidence. I have found that the activities included in this book have really helped children to enjoy their work, to learn and also have fun at the same time – a real boost for self-esteem! I hope other practitioners will find the same.

The book is not intended as a definitive guide to all the ideas and resources there are, neither is it an academic book. It is an account of lessons and activities that have worked well for colleagues and me. The views and opinions expressed are solely mine, based on my experience in teaching and because of this I have not attempted to justify them with examples of academic research.

All the activities can be carried out in a school setting, either in the classroom or the hall. My own experience has been with children from Foundation Stage to Year 3 and so the way the activities are approached changes, depending on the age and ability of the children. I see no reason why they cannot also be adapted and changed to benefit older children and I have indicated which activities might work particularly well in Key Stage 2. Teachers can adapt the activities to suit their children and their own settings.

I have tried to organise the book so that it is clear and easy to use. The DfES/QCA recent guidance for schools: *Speaking, Listening, Learning: Working with Children in Key Stages 1 and 2* (2003) mentions techniques that some of the activities I have used come under. Schools should have received this pack, which gives examples of how speaking and listening can fit across the curriculum. It includes teaching objectives for Years 1 to 6, covering the four strands of the National Curriculum for speaking and listening. It also shows some links to the NLS (National Literacy Strategy).

I have included some of the objectives from that guidance; the objective number shown is the same as that in the guidance. Some NLS objectives are also included, plus some of the relevant stepping stones from the *Guidance for the Foundation Stage*. These are only suggestions as to which objectives I think best fit the activities; you may think of some others. Much of the word-level work from the NLS should be covered through ongoing phonics teaching and so I have only included word-level objectives if they are particularly relevant to an activity. Where appropriate, reference is made to the Primary National Strategy (PNS) objectives. If there are no objectives for a particular year group ascribed to an activity, this does not mean you cannot use that activity with that year group. All these activities are good for developing language whatever the age of the children. How you approach them will vary. The 'aims' in each section relate, in general, to the National Curriculum objectives in the programme of study for speaking and listening. However, I have added some aims of my own where appropriate.

I have mentioned opportunities for assessment with some of the activities. Most of the activities described here involve speaking and listening as part of a lesson; it is up to individual teachers what the focus of the lesson is. If the focus is speaking or listening then the children will need to be given a clear speaking or listening – learning intention, with success criteria from which assessment can be made.

The book is arranged in chapters describing and explaining the activities. Some sections include photocopiable materials if relevant and they all show cross-curricular links and ideas for planning when the activities can be carried out. In the cross-curricular section I have, in some cases, indicated precisely how the activity might fit in across the curriculum. There is a list of resources required although some of the activities do not need any. By arranging the book in this way, everything required for a particular activity can be found in one place. Practitioners can turn to the activity they wish and 'lift' the whole section, which should include all the information they need. A section is included in the reference section at the end of the book naming titles of books and resources that I have found particularly helpful and that children have responded to really well. These are only suggestions and do not have to be used. Some suggestions of how teaching assistants might be deployed are also included.

There is no recommended order for these activities to be carried out. If they are being planned as a unit of work in the literacy hour, some activities may need to precede others as a means of introduction to the following work. I will mention this when necessary. I would suggest that the best way to start is to choose an activity that does not appear too daunting and have a go. Do not worry at the start about tying it into the curriculum. You will need to do this eventually but it is important to build your confidence first. Be positive and have confidence in yourself. Children are very forgiving and although you might think you are making a complete fool of yourself when you are in 'role', or with a puppet on your arm, your average 5- and 6-year-olds will think it's great!

I am aware that many teachers have a bank of activities that work well for them and are confident to use them, in which case I hope they might find at least one or two ideas here that they have not tried before! For those who are less confident and are unsure about implementing activities that include speaking and listening, I hope they will be encouraged and inspired to try some of those mentioned in this book.

I once heard it said 'a silent classroom is not natural'. When I think of the learning and progress I have seen when children are engaged in meaningful discourse and language activities, I have to agree!

Activities around songs, poetry and rhymes

This chapter includes:

- ■ Activities using songs and nursery rhymes

- ■ Poetry, including alliteration, syllables and rhyme

- ■ A reminder of some of the old favourite action songs and rhymes.

Before trying these activities, here is an interesting exercise to start with.

Make a list of all the nursery rhymes you can remember from your own childhood. I did this recently and came up with 58 in ten minutes.

After you have done that, have a thinking session with your class and see how many they can think of collectively. My class of 29 Year 1s thought of 17, which falls quite a bit short of my score.

I did this because I thought it might give an indication of how much previous exposure the children in the class might have had to nursery rhymes. It is my experience that often the children who know lots of nursery rhymes are the ones whose speech and language are more developed. These children also seem to acquire other literacy skills more readily. In addition to this, nursery rhymes are fun and enjoyable to recite and they can help to boost the confidence of more reserved children.

Activity 1 – Share a rhyme or song

Aims – To encourage participation, build confidence, enhance listening skills, identify and respond to sound patterns in language.

What to do – Ask the class if anyone is brave enough to stand up and say a rhyme. (There is always at least one taker, and usually more!) Make sure the rest of the class are listening, and explain that they are the audience and must listen really carefully. It is a good idea to explain that no one must laugh or make fun of their friends. When the child has said their rhyme, make sure everyone claps and gives lots of praise.

Resources required – None.

Cross curricular links – Music, literacy.

When to do it – As a stand-alone activity fitted in to any time in the day where there are a few minutes to spare such as waiting to go home at the end of the day or just before lunch while waiting for dinner ladies to arrive, or as part of a music lesson. In literacy as part of a unit of work on rhymes or poetry.

Use of teaching assistants – Encourage children to listen while their friends are reciting. Suggest ideas and quietly encourage less confident children to have a go. Confident teaching assistants may be willing to run similar sessions themselves, either with groups or the whole class if an opportunity arises.

NLS and Foundation Stage objectives

Foundation Stage – Communication, language and literacy

Linking sounds and letters
Enjoy rhyming and rhythmic activities.
Show awareness of rhyme and alliteration.
Recognise rhythm in spoken words.

Language for communication
Listen to favourite nursery rhymes and songs. Join in with repeated refrains, anticipating key events and important phrases.

NLS Year R

Word level
W1 To understand and be able to rhyme through:

● recognising, exploring and working with rhyming patterns, e.g. learning nursery rhymes.

Text level
T10 To re-read and recite stories and rhymes with predictable and repeated patterns and experiment with similar rhyming patterns.

Further comments and suggestions – I have found that even the most reticent of children will find the courage to stand up and recite a familiar nursery rhyme. I never *make* children take part but it is surprising how children who are usually very quiet and shy often want to have a go. One way of encouraging them is to let them do it with a friend. I will also help a child out by quietly reminding them of the words if they get stuck.

An adaptation of this is to let the children sing a song of their choice. This can work really well if the children's home experiences are with modern pop culture, rather than along the more traditional one of nursery rhymes. It enables them to participate with more confidence and shows that their interests and home experiences are valued. In these situations you may find, like me, that you are unable to 'help out' if they get stuck, but plenty of their classmates can!

Older children may also respond better to singing a pop song rather then a nursery rhyme. I recently saw three Year 3 girls, one of whom is very shy, stand in front of the whole school and perform their own rendering of a Madonna song.

Poetry

Poetry is a brilliant way of encouraging use of language and words and can be approached in a way that makes it lively and interesting for children. Not only can it help them develop an ear for rhyme and sounds but it can also have a huge effect on writing. It is important to let children explore the possibilities of poetry and rhyme so that they develop a positive attitude towards it from the very start. There is scope in the NLS to play with poetry and it can be planned into the literacy hour in a fun way, quite easily. It should be noted that I used these activities in a unit of work on poetry, which included reading and writing.

Listening to others is an important part of developing language skills and young children need to listen to plenty of poems. You can make a tape of the children's favourite poems and rhymes for them to listen to as an activity for literacy. This might include poems recited by yourself, TAs, other willing adults or a tape made from the children's own recitations: children love to listen to themselves speaking. Take time to read poems to the children yourself. They particularly like listening to poems that are slightly subversive or silly, such as those by Colin McNaughton, Michael Rosen and Roald Dahl. I find children will ask for their favourite poems over and over again and begin to learn them by heart. You can hear them practising them, self-correcting and trying again as they go off to play or to lunch.

Which poems are used depends to some extent on personal preference. A poetry session is going to work much better if the teacher is enthused and knowledgeable about the material they are using. Not all poems suit all teachers: we all have our own favourites.

The activities I have described here are light-hearted, playing with rhyme and alliteration. Riddles, limericks and tongue-twisters are all kinds of poetry that appeal to children through humour.

It is not essential to do this activity before the next one but older children may find it useful if they are trying to make a rhyme 'fit'. I do not use this activity on its own but within a unit of work on poetry. I usually plan a lesson on syllables to help the children understand the rhythm of some poems.

Activity 2 – Sorting syllables

Aims – To identify and respond to sound patterns in language.

What to do – Explain that words have a beat (like in music). Introduce the idea of syllables by clapping the syllables in your own name. Try getting the children to clap their names. Help them by giving examples. For example, in the name Connor there are two syllables,

Con and *or*. Ask the children to say the syllables in their name as they clap them and share it with their talk partners.

When you feel the children have a reasonable idea of syllables, choose a poem with a steady rhythm and beat; 'Twinkle, Twinkle, Little Star' is a good one. Ask the children to do the same as they did with their names only with each line of the poem. This particular poem has seven syllables in each line of all the verses (apart from the third line of the third verse and the second line of the fourth verse), which is why it has a steady rhythm. Write the number of syllables up on the board as you do each line. The children will soon spot the pattern.

Resources required – A copy of 'Twinkle, Twinkle Little Star', all verses, preferably in a big book format; see Spotlight on Poetry. *Classic Poems 1* (1999), or any poem with a strong rhythm. Pen to write the syllable tally per line.

Cross-curricular links – Music.

When to do it – In the literacy hour as part of a unit of work on poetry. As part of a music lesson, as a fun way to dismiss the children for lunch, break or home time.

Use of teaching assistants – Ask them to count on their fingers as you clap the syllables and say them with the children (it can be tricky trying to count while sounding the syllables at the same time). Support the children as they work out the syllables in their names. Work in a small group situation with those children who might be struggling.

NLS and Foundation Stage objectives

Foundation Stage – Communication, language and literacy

Linking sounds and letters
Enjoy rhyming and rhythmic activities.
Recognise rhythm in spoken words.

Year 2 Term 2

Word level
W5 To discriminate, orally, syllables in multi-syllabic words using children's names and words from their reading, e.g. *dinosaur*, *family*, *dinner*, *children*. Extend to written forms and note syllabic boundary in speech and writing.

Year 2 Term 3

Word level
W2 To reinforce work on discriminating syllables in reading and spelling from previous term.

Year 3 Terms 1, 2, 3

Word level
W4 To discriminate syllables in reading and spelling (from Year 2).

Further comments and suggestions – Children generally love this activity. Some will find it difficult to distinguish the syllables even after lots of practice, particularly if you are working with younger children.

It will of course depend on the age and ability of the children and when in the school year you do it as to how you approach it. Foundation Stage and Year 1 transition issues should also be considered. Some children in the Foundation Stage will be able to hear the syllables easily and follow and clap a rhythm, while some in Year 1 can't.

It should be mentioned that the term 'syllable' does not occur in the NLS until Year 2 term 2. This does not mean that it cannot be used before. Children love 'big' words and there is no harm in dropping it in if it is appropriate; you need to use your knowledge of your own class to decide. The activity works well with Years 2 and 3 but I have used it successfully with Year 1.

Activity 3 – Silly rhymes

Aims – To speak clearly with appropriate intonation, choose words with precision and organise what is said, listen to other's reactions, identify and respond to sound patterns in language, encourage appropriate responses.

What to do – Explain that you are going to show the children how to use a familiar poem or nursery rhyme to make up their own. Read some examples of rhymes that have been changed from the original, such as Michael Rosen's 'Humpty Dumpty Went to the Moon,' 'Twinkle Twinkle Little Bat' by Lewis Carroll or something similar; there are lots of examples.

Next, read one or two nursery rhymes that you have decided to use so that the children are reminded of the original.

Show the children what you want them to do by modelling it. It is a good idea to have thought of some examples of your own beforehand and to have worked out how you might change them. Keep it simple to start with. Try just changing the last few words of the first two lines, e.g.

> *Humpty Dumpty sat on a star,*
> *Humpty Dumpty did not go far!*

You may find you need to provide more models before the children get the idea – it will depend on your class. When you are modelling it explain what you are doing and why. Get the children to help you think of words to use.

Let the children go away in pairs and try to think of their own silly rhymes. You will need to move around the class while they are doing this to ensure they are on task and to mediate in any disputes. Some children can find it quite challenging even to think of one word to rhyme with another word. I usually pair the children with their talk partners so that they can support each other, and it is also more fun to work with a friend. At the end of the session come together and share the rhymes. Encourage the children to listen carefully to their friends' contributions. They can laugh with their friends but not at them.

Finally take ideas and write them on the board. If children have an idea about syllables it can help them when they try to think of a rhyming second line to fit. Older children in particular may find this useful, which is why it may help if the previous activity is carried out before this one.

Resources required – Any big book of nursery rhymes, a copy of some examples of rhymes that have been changed.

Cross-curricular links – Music, literacy.

When to do it – In the literacy hour planned as part of a poetry unit; as part of a music lesson

Use of teaching assistants – Support individuals and selected groups of children.

NLS and Foundation Stage objectives

Foundation Stage – Communication, language and literacy

Linking sounds and letters
Enjoy rhyming and rhythmic activities.
Show awareness or rhyme and alliteration.
Recognise rhyme in spoken words.
Continuing a rhyming string.

Language for communication
Enjoy listening to and using spoken written language, and readily turn it into play and learning.

Sustain attentive listening, responding to what they have heard by relevant comments, questions or actions.

Listen with enjoyment, and respond to stories, songs and other music, rhymes and poems and make up their own stories, songs, rhymes and poems.

Reception Year

Word level
W1 To understand and be able to rhyme through:

- recognising, exploring and working with rhyming patterns, e.g. learning nursery rhymes
- extending these patterns by analogy, generating new and invented words in speech and spelling.

Text level
T10 To re-read and recite stories and rhymes with predictable and repeated patterns and experiment with similar rhyming patterns.

Year 1 Term 1

Word level

W1 From YR, to practise and secure the ability to rhyme and to relate this to spelling patterns through:

- exploring and playing with rhyming patterns.

Text level

T6 To recite stories and rhymes with predictable and repeating patterns, extemporising on patterns orally by substituting words and phrases, extending patterns, inventing patterns and playing with rhyme.

Year 1 Term 2

Text level

T13 To substitute and extend patterns from reading through play, e.g. by using same lines and introducing new words, extending lines or alliterative patterns, adding further rhyming words, lines.

Year 2 Term 1

Text level

T7 To learn, re-read and recite favourite poems, taking account of punctuation; to comment on aspects such as word combinations, sound patterns (such as rhymes, rhythms, alliterative patterns) and forms of presentation.

T12 To use simple poetry structures and to substitute own ideas, write new lines.

Year 2 Term 2

Word level

T8 Read own poems aloud.

T9 To identify and discuss patterns of rhythm, rhyme and other features of sound in different poems.

Year 2 Term 3

Text level

T8 To discuss meaning of words and phrases that create humour, and sound effects in poetry, e.g. nonsense poems, tongue-twisters, riddles, and to classify poems into simple types; to make class anthologies.

Year 3 Term 3

Text level

T7 To select, prepare, read aloud and recite by heart poetry that plays with language or entertains; to recognise rhyme, alliteration and other patterns of sound that create effects.

Further comments and suggestions – These rhymes may seem silly but children love making them up and reciting them. It encourages children to think of words and use them in different ways and in unusual contexts, as well as developing an awareness of rhyme.

By its very silliness this becomes a non-threatening activity and less confident children often feel more able to join in. If rhymes are a little 'naughty' then all the better, as I found out when two small boys came up with:

> *Humpty Dumpty sat on the sun*
> *Humpty Dumpty burnt his bum!*

These boys were often reluctant to engage in literacy activities but really enjoyed this one!

Here are some other examples of rhymes that I have used and how the children changed them. These are all the children's own work.

> *Hickory Dickory Dock,*
> *The mouse fell off the clock,*
> *The clock struck seven*
> *The mouse went to heaven.*
> *Hickory Dickory Dock.*

> *Hey Diddle Diddle*
> *The cat and the fiddle*
> *The spider gave him a push*
> *The little dog laughed to see such fun*
> *And the cat fell into a bush.*

A common problem can be that some children find it very difficult to hear the rhyme in words and in these cases a lot of support and encouragement will be required. These children are often the ones who struggle to acquire literacy skills.

The PIPS (Progression in Phonics) activity 'The Pebble Game' is a good activity for helping with this problem. It helps in raising awareness of rhyme and the ability to create and continue different rhyming strings. How to play this game (and many other phonic games) is explained in the *Progression in Phonics* handbook or if this is not available on the CD-ROM in the professional development resource pack from the DfES – Ref: DfES 0213-2003.

Activity 4 – Reading/reciting with expression

Aims – To encourage participation, enhance listening skills, sustain concentration, develop confidence in speaking aloud and speak with clear diction and appropriate intonation, taking into account the needs of listeners.

What to do – Read a short poem twice, first with expression, and then without. Ask the children to tell you which style they liked the best and why. The response of the children will depend on your class, but at least one child will say they preferred the recitation spoken with expression, even if they find it hard to say why.

Next, explain that they are going to try reading some poems with expression. You should confirm that the children know what you mean by 'expression'. It will depend on the age and ability of the children how you do this activity. If the children are older or reasonably fluent readers you might let them choose a poem of their own choice to recite or read. For others it is an idea to select a poem for them or let them choose a favourite nursery rhyme.

Give the children time to practise their piece and then ask them to read it to the class. As always in these kinds of activities, be aware that some children may be reluctant to participate so treat this sensitively.

Resources required – Selected poetry books or nursery rhymes for the children to read from.

Cross-curricular links – Literacy.

When to do it – In the literacy hour within a unit of work on poetry, narrative or as in Activity 1, during odd spare minutes of the day such as waiting to go home or for the arrival of dinner ladies.

Use of teaching assistants – Encourage children to listen while their friends are reciting. Suggest ideas and quietly encourage less confident children to have a go. Confident teaching assistants may be willing to run similar sessions themselves, either with groups or the whole class if an opportunity arises.

NLS and Foundation Stage objectives

Foundation Stage – Communication, language and literacy

Language for communication
Enjoy listening to and using spoken written language, and readily turn to it in their play and learning.

Sustain attentive listening, responding to what they have heard with relevant comments questions or actions.

Listen with enjoyment, and respond to stories, songs and other music, rhymes and poems and make up their own stories, songs, rhymes and poems.

Year 1 Term 1

Sentence level
S3 To draw on grammatical awareness, to read with appropriate expression and intonation, e.g. in reading to others, or to dolls, puppets.

Year 1 Term 2

Text level
T11 To learn and recite simple poems and rhymes, with actions, and to re-read them from the text.

Year 1 Term 3

Sentence level

S3 To read familiar texts aloud with pace and expression appropriate to the grammar, e.g. pausing at full stops, raising voice for questions.

Year 2 Term 1

Sentence level

S3 To recognise and take account of commas and exclamation marks in reading aloud with appropriate expression.

Text level

T7 To learn, re-read and recite favourite poems, taking account of punctuation; to comment on aspects such as word combinations, sound patterns (such as rhymes, rhythms, alliterative patterns) and forms of presentation.

Year 2 Term 2

Sentence level

S2 To read aloud with intonation and expression appropriate to the grammar and punctuation (sentences, speech marks, exclamation marks).

Text level

T10 To comment on and recognise when the reading aloud of a poem makes sense and is effective.

Year 2 Term 3

Sentence level

S1 To read text aloud with intonation and expression appropriate to the grammar and punctuation.

Year 3 Term 1

Sentence level

S2 To take account of the grammar and punctuation, e.g. sentences, speech marks, exclamation marks and commas to mark pauses, when reading aloud.

Year 3 Term 2

Text level

T4 To choose and prepare poems for performance, identifying appropriate expression, tone, volume and use of voices and other sounds.

T5 Rehearse and improve performance, taking note of punctuation and meaning.

Year 3 Term 3

Text level

T7 To select, prepare, read aloud and recite by heart poetry that plays with language or entertains; to recognise rhyme, alliteration and other patterns of sound that create effects.

PNS objectives — Speaking, listening, learning

Year 2 term 1

13. Speaking

To speak with clarity and use intonation when reading and reciting texts, e.g. learning choral techniques to emphasise rhythm and meaning.

Link with NLS text objective 7.

Year 3 term 2

29. Speaking

To choose and prepare poems or stories for performance, identifying appropriate expression, tone, volume and use of voices and other sounds, e.g. presenting poems from other cultures using intonation to interpret punctuation and emphasise meaning.

Link with NLS text objectives 4 and 5.

Further comments and suggestions — The best way for children to understand the importance and effect of reading with expression is for the teacher to model it, if necessary more than once. Be warned: it can be surprisingly hard to read a piece of poetry or narrative without expression when you are used to doing it otherwise.

A problem that I always encounter when using nursery rhymes is that children tend to sing rather than say them. It can take a bit of practice and a few attempts to get it right. This problem obviously does not happen if the children are reciting poems rather than familiar rhymes.

I have had some excellent recitations, and recently listened to a child who struggles with literacy read 'Mary, Mary Quite Contrary' with lovely expression and intonation. He interpreted it beautifully. This was a real boost for a child lacking in confidence and self-esteem.

This activity is good for all ages but can be used to really good effect with older children, or those reading fluently enough to tackle more challenging expressive poems. It can also be used in the same way for reading prose when teaching narrative as part of the literacy hour.

Activity 5 — Playing with alliteration

Aims — To speak clearly with appropriate intonation, choose words with precision and organise what is said, listen to others' reactions, identify and respond to sound patterns in language, encourage appropriate responses.

What to do — Explain to the children what alliteration is. Give them some examples by modelling it, e.g. 'Cute Connor cut the cake' and 'Terrific Timmy tooted on his tuba'.

Next, ask the children to do the same and think of a sentence that has as many words that begin with the same letter as possible, such as, 'Jolly Jasmine jumped in a jelly!' Try to use their names in your explanation as children always respond well to activities that relate to them personally.

Ask them to think of and share their ideas with their talk partners and then share them with the whole class. Discuss those that worked well and why.

This can be used as a group activity when you are reasonably confident that the children have got the idea (see further comments and suggestions).

Resources required – Tape recorders, audiotapes, examples of alliteration in poetry and tongue-twisters such as 'Peter Piper' and 'Betty bought a bit of butter'.

Cross-Curricular links – ICT, literacy.

When to do it – In the literacy hour planned as part of a poetry unit.

Use of teaching assistants – Encourage and support less confident children during whole-class input. Work with groups to support and encourage ideas, mediate with groups who struggle to work co-operatively.

NLS and Foundation Stage objectives

Foundation Stage – Communication, language and literacy

Linking sounds and letters
Enjoy rhyming and rhythmic activities.
Show awareness or rhyme and alliteration.

Language for communication
Enjoy listening to and using spoken written language, and readily turn it into play and learning.

Sustain attentive listening, responding to what they have heard by relevant comments, questions or actions.

Listen with enjoyment, and respond to stories, songs and other music, rhymes and poems and make up their own stories, songs, rhymes and poems.

Reception Year

Word level
W4 To link sound and spelling patterns by:

● identifying alliteration in known and new and invented words.

Year 2 Term 1

Text level
T7 To learn, re-read and recite favourite poems, taking account of punctuation; to comment on aspects such as word combinations, sound patterns (such as rhymes, rhythms alliterative patterns) and forms of presentation.

Year 2 Term 2

Text level

T9 To identify and discuss patterns of rhythm, rhyme and other features of sound in different poems.

Year 3 Term 3

Text level

T7 To select, prepare, read aloud and recite by heart poetry that plays with language or entertains; to recognise rhyme, alliteration and other patterns of sound that create effects.

Further comments and suggestions – I have used this activity with 5- to 8-year-olds as an independent group activity. The children think of an alliterative sentence, just as they did as a whole class with their talk partners. When they have thought of their sentence and practised saying it to their group, they take turns to say it into the tape recorder. This usually proves to be really popular, as children like to hear themselves on tape in the same way they like to see themselves in photos and on videos.

This activity can be used in the early years although younger children may need assistance in using the recorder. In the Foundation Stage and Year 1 children enjoy playing with words and sounds so why not let them use alliteration, despite the fact it does not come into the NLS until Year 2 term 1? The same principle applies here as mentioned in Activity 2: some children will be able to make alliterative sentences at a younger age and thoroughly enjoy it. Use the activity as best suits your class and the stage they are at and enjoy it.

When carrying out this task the children will need to be briefed on how to behave and they need to be clear about your expectations. To avoid arguments appoint one child to be in charge of the tape recorder. He or she can then turn it on, as each child in the group is ready.

Using recordings of children's oral work both in this activity and others has a number of advantages. You can use their recordings in the plenary to reinforce your learning intention, and it is also a record of how they coped. It can be used as an assessment of their understanding and gives you a clear idea of who managed the task. You could also use it as a speaking and listening assessment. Be prepared for lots of laughing and giggling if you play it back to the whole class; they love it. It is also a very effective way to encourage listening because they all want to hear themselves. Children can become confused between rhyming words and alliteration. It is not unusual for them to think of sentences such as 'little Luke sat on a hat.' Listening to tapes of children's oral activities can help identify misconceptions like this and can be used to determine the learning objective of future lessons.

An adaptation of this could be to get the children to say rhyming strings into the tape recorder or indeed the silly rhymes from Activity 3.

A nice everyday activity with alliteration is to try to alliterate the children's names such as, Lovely Lewis, Marvellous Mitchell, and Happy Holly. This idea can then be reinforced by playing the PIPS game 'Jingles'. Alliterating their names is a simple thing to do but the children love it and will try to think of their own ideas. It can be done for fun when lining them up for playtime, lunch, and assembly or at other times. It all helps to get children thinking of words and how to use language in a way that is fun and accessible.

Older children who have had some experience of alliteration should be taught that it is often used in poetry to emphasise mood and atmosphere as well as for creating tongue twisters.

Action songs and games

I finish this chapter with a brief mention of action songs and games. These are many and varied and are excellent for involving children and encouraging them to participate, take turns, etc. There are alphabet songs and number songs – the list is endless. Don't forget all the old favourites such as, 'The Farmer's in his Den', 'In and Out the Dusty Bluebells', 'Ring a Ring o' Roses', 'Down by the Station', 'I'm a Little Teapot', 'Five Little Men in a Flying Saucer', 'This Old Man', 'Miss Polly had a Dolly', 'One, Two, Three, Four, Five', 'Five Current Buns', and 'Here we go Looby Lou' to name just a few.

Take time to search the shelves of your local bookshop or library and you will find books with both old and new rhymes and games in them. A list of some titles I have found useful is included in the reference section at the end of this book.

Home corners and talk areas

This chapter includes:
How to set up role-play areas for:

- A shop

- A castle

- A home corner

- Thoughts on the diversity of classroom talk

- Opportunities for encouraging talk in areas of the curriculum such as art and history.

Traditionally called 'home corners,' role-play areas, as well as replicating the home environment, can be rearranged to emulate a wide range of different settings. The opportunities for talk within these areas are phenomenal and they can be used for both structured activities and free play. When children are left to play without restraints they often draw on personal experience that is important to their social and linguistic development. Imaginative play allows children to experiment with and act out life experiences in a safe environment. Children who are usually very quiet are often less inhibited when playing with friends in the role-play area. I recently heard a colleague comment about a little girl in her class saying, 'I have never heard Amy talk so much, she normally never says a word!' The child was playing in the home corner.

A role-play area can also provide contexts for other literacy skills such as reading and writing. Children might read stories to dolls and their friends and write letters, shopping lists, or invitations to a pretend party.

Most of the principles for setting up one role-play area can be applied to another and even the procedure of planning and setting up an area promotes discussion which helps develop language skills. Some ideas for role-play areas might include a doctor's surgery; this can easily be adapted to a vet's. Other ideas could include a post office, a cinema, an airport, a fast-food outlet and so on.

'Real life' role-play areas

Activity 1 – Make a shop

Aims – To promote discussion, enhance listening skills, help develop appropriate related vocabulary, e.g. buy, sell, counter, customer, shop assistant, change, till, etc., take turns in speaking, make relevant comments.

What to do – Explain to the children what they will be doing and take ideas for what type of shop they would like. It is good to include them because it will give them more ownership of the whole activity. You may have your own plans or preferences but one child is bound to come up with something similar to what you have in mind. Some suggestions might be: a book shop, toy shop, sweet shop on its own or as a newsagents, a green grocer or a supermarket or corner shop that would sell a little of everything.

When you have decided on the type of shop, begin to collect items to go in it. A lot of things can be begged and borrowed from within school; most infant schools should have items such as tills and plastic money readily available. Don't forget parents, who are often willing to help if asked.

Some props can be made, e.g. sweets out of pastry, Play-Doh™ or plasticine, fruit and vegetables out of papier mâché. Boxes can also be made from card, although it is easy enough to collect old packaging if you start well before you need the shop. Don't forget the sweet wrappers!

Get the children to help make a stripy shop awning. It makes a great display and adds to the feel of the shop.

If you decide to make a newsagents or bookshop, don't forget to include any newspapers or books that the children may have made themselves. Trawl different classes and ask to borrow any 'publications' that other children have produced. This really makes the play area 'their own'. Remember, all this preparation will involve extensive dialogue, discussion and possibly some negotiation.

Resources required – These will depend on the sort of shop you choose. Here are some suggestions for those shops mentioned. All the shops will require shelves or stands, till, plastic money, table for the counter, stickers or cards for price labels.

Bookshop
Collection of different sorts of books, adult, children's, fiction and non-fiction, hardback and paperback.

Toy shop
Collection of assorted toys and games.

Sweetshop and newsagents
Papers, comics and magazines (real and made by children). Make sure the papers and magazines you use have no articles or pictures that parents might object to their children looking at. Paperback books for adults and children, greetings cards, pretend sweets and chocolate.

Greengrocer
Collection of plastic fruit and vegetables; to increase amount include children's own papier mâché ones. Try to include more unusual fruit and vegetables, particularly if your class has children from different ethnic backgrounds. Find out from them, or their parents, which fruits and vegetables they eat that other children might not be familiar with. This will make them feel their culture is being recognised and valued and is a great talking point.

Supermarket or corner shop
Many of the items mentioned for the other shops could be included in a supermarket. As well as those include plastic pretend food. Most schools have these for the home corner, e.g. canned food, fish, bread, butter, cheese and milk. Once again, if you cannot find plastic ones get the children to make them. If you can get hold of one or two of the little play supermarket trolleys available all the better, but dolls' prams make a good substitute.

Cross-curricular links – Maths, art and design, DT, history, literacy.

When to do it –

Maths – in using and applying number, calculations, solving numerical problems and work with money.

Art and design – in exploring and developing ideas.

Design and technology – making sweets, fruit and vegetables, designing and making wrappers, and awning, in developing, planning and communicating ideas.

History – as part of a topic on changes in knowledge and understanding of events, people and changes in the past. A shop that replicates shops in the past would also fit in well as a project for certain aspects of history at Key Stage 2.

Literacy – within units of work such as stories with related themes and stories with familiar settings. Texts such as Shirley Hughes's *Alfie and Annie Rose* and *Lucy and Tom* stories are particularly good. A shop could also be linked to some of the non-fiction units.

Use of teaching assistants – to oversee groups in the play area, to make observations and listen to the language and vocabulary used to report back to the teacher, to remind older children of the learning objectives, to lead and participate in a group activity if specifically directed by the teacher. For example, in maths helping children to use subtraction to work out change, to dress up and go into role as part of the group. A confident teaching assistant may be willing to oversee the rest of the class as they get on with their group or individual tasks to allow the teacher to work with the group in the role-play area.

NLS and Foundation Stage objectives

Foundation Stage – Communication, language, and literacy

Language for communication
Listen to others in one-to-one/small groups when conversation interests them.

Enjoy listening to and using spoken language and readily turn to it in their play and learning.

Interact with others, negotiating plans and activities and taking turns in conversation.

Language for thinking
Begin to use talk to pretend imaginary situations.

Use language to imagine and recreate roles and experiences.

Creative development

Engage in imaginative role-play based on own first-hand experiences.

Play alongside other children who are engaged in the same theme.

Play co-operatively as part of a group to act out a narrative.

Year 1 Term 1

Text level
T7 To re-enact stories in a variety of ways, e.g. through role-play, using dolls or puppets.

Year 2 Term 2

Text level
T7 To prepare and re-tell stories individually and through role-play in groups, using dialogue and narrative from text.

PNS objectives – Speaking, listening and learning

Year 1 Term 1

4. Drama
To explore familiar themes and characters through improvisation and role-play, e.g. using story boxes and bags of props to create characters.

Link with NLS text objective 7.

Year 1 Term 2

8. Drama
To act out own and well-known stories, using different voices for characters, i.e. using drama techniques to portray characters and motives.

Link with NLS text objectives 9 and 15.

Further comments and suggestions – A shop (or any role-play area) will fit easily into the various focuses of the early years. The Foundation curriculum has a strong emphasis on the importance of learning, through play, and it is easier for all the children to have the opportunity to use the role-play area than in Key Stages 1 and 2. Practitioners should include opportunities for play in their long-term plans, ensuring that some of the language and literacy objectives for the early learning goals are covered.

Although making the shop is relatively easy, it is harder to plan to use it at Key Stage 1, and even more so at Key Stage 2 because the curriculum is so full. One alternative is to plan for groups to use it during independent work time. You will need to keep a record of which groups have been in it to ensure everybody gets a turn. You will also need to decide what you want the children to learn from using it.

Most children love to use the role-play area and older children will use it providing the activity is approached in a way that is appropriate to their age group and learning experience.

Play areas that children can relate to are important; it is no good making a theatre and booking office if only a limited number of children have experienced this. Children cannot role-play real-life situations they have not experienced or know nothing about.

This was illustrated for me recently as I listened to a conversation about role-play. A restaurant had been set up but the children were unable to use it because for most of them it was outside their experience. The teacher arranged for them to see what happens in a real restaurant and after that they role-played brilliantly, with waiters taking orders, seating customers, and customers looking at menus and ordering food and asking for the bill and paying it.

'Imaginary' role-play areas

Activity 2 – Make a castle

Aims – To encourage participation, promote discussion, enhance listening skills, help develop use of appropriate related vocabulary, e.g. words to do fairy tales such as knight, prince, dragon, princess; also technical words such as moat, keep, battlements and drawbridge, etc.; take turns in speaking, make relevant comments.

What to do – As with the other activities, explain to the children what you (and they) are going to do. This particular area can be used in a totally imaginary way, relating to fairy stories, myths and legends, or in a factual way if using it with older children at Key Stage 2, in connection with a unit of history work. How you approach it and your expectations will depend to some extent on the age of the children. You will need to establish how much the children already know about castles, which will depend on their previous work, knowledge and understanding.

First have a class discussion about castles. This topic should generate a real buzz of enthusiasm as the children get caught up in it. It might be the bloodthirsty side of life in a castle that grabs them, or the magical fantasy side – either way they will not be short of things to say.

Next, ask the children to talk with their talk partners to discuss what things could go in the castle. Try, as unobtrusively as possible, to listen to the discussions without joining in. This can give a real insight into the level of talk the children are engaging in and which children are contributing. This applies to all these activities.

Afterwards take their suggestions and ideas and as a class decide which will be the most practical to use. Once this has been decided you can start to put it together. As with the shop, some of the props can be made. You will find if you make a point of listening, that a lot of talk is generated while the children are involved in making props such as the castle walls.

Resources required – Clothes that can be adapted or changed to different outfits, a suggestion of castle walls or battlements (card can be cut and painted appropriately); if the area is to be used as a fairy tale setting then items that represent jewels, a wand, witch's broom, cauldron, etc. Many of your resources will depend on what the children decide should be included.

Cross-curricular links – History, literacy, geography, DT and art and design.

When to do it – As a focus for independent group work, or as a group activity including an adult in an active role.

Literacy – within a unit of work on fairy stories, fantasy worlds, myths, legends, and adventure stories. Non-fiction – within a unit of work on information books, recounts of observations, visits and events, explanations.

History – under 'knowledge and understanding of events, people and changes in the past', 'historical enquiry' or a local history study.

Geography – sites of castles could be included within 'geographical enquiry and skills', and 'knowledge and understanding of places'.

Design and technology – making props under 'developing, planning and communicating ideas', 'working with tools, equipment, materials and components to make quality products'.

Art & Design – using castles as a theme of work (see the 'Take one picture' website referred to in Chapter 6).

Use of teaching assistants – As in previous activity.

NLS and Foundation Stage objectives

Foundation Stage – Communication, language and literacy

Language for communication
Listen to others in one-to-one/small groups when conversation interests them.

Enjoy listening to and using spoken language and readily turn to it in their play and learning.

Interact with others, negotiating plans and activities and taking turns in conversation.

Language for thinking
Begin to use talk to pretend imaginary situations.

Use language to imagine and recreate roles and experiences.

Creative development
Engage in imaginative role-play based on own first-hand experiences.

Play alongside other children who are engaged in the same theme.

Play co-operatively as part of a group to act out a narrative.

Year 1 Term 1

Text level
T7 To re-enact stories in a variety of ways, e.g. through role-play, using dolls or puppets.

Year1 Term 2

Text level
T9 To become aware of character and dialogue, e.g. by role-playing parts when reading aloud stories or plays with others.

Year 2 Term 2

Text level
T7 To prepare and re-tell stories individually and through role-play in groups, using dialogue and narrative from text.

NPS objectives – Speaking, listening and learning

Year 1 Term 1

4. Drama
To explore familiar themes and characters through improvisation and role-play, e.g. using story boxes and bags of props to create characters.

Link with NLS text objective 7.

Year 1 Term 2

8. Drama
To act out own and well-known stories, using different voices for characters, i.e. using drama techniques to portray characters and motives.

Link with NLS text objectives 9 and 15.

Further comments and suggestions – You may try relating this to films the children have seen like 'Shrek', or one of the numerous versions of 'Robin Hood' such as the Disney cartoon. Most children are familiar with film and television and visual stimulus is an excellent tool for generating discussion and use of the imagination. Children whose literacy experiences may be limited will often respond well to a visual stimulus.

Home corners

So far I have described a variety themes for role-play areas, which can be used across the curriculum. The traditional 'home corner' also provides an excellent setting and stimulus for talk such as mother and baby talk, telephone conversations, etc., and as already mentioned the opportunity for reading and writing. All children whatever their background can relate to an area where they can 'play' being at home because it is within their immediate experience.

The home backgrounds of children from different ethnic groups should also be considered. Try to collect a variety of clothes and cooking utensils other than those that are Western European. The children will love to try on the different clothes and they provide a great focus for talk. It can give EAL (English as an additional language) children a chance to answer questions about something they are familiar with, and to take the lead in discussions. It also shows that their culture is being recognised and valued.

As we have seen with the previous activities, the setting up of a role-play area provides lots of opportunity for talk and discussion. This applies even more when the area is very familiar to them because even children with limited experiences of life outside home and school are able to contribute.

Most teachers, I expect, are very familiar with the nature of a home corner but for those who might not be I have included setting up a home corner as an activity.

Activity 3 – Make a home corner

Aims – To promote discussion, enhance listening skills, help develop everyday vocabulary and communication, take turns in speaking, make relevant comments.

What to do – Explain to the children that you want their help to set up a home corner. If there is already a home corner then a discussion could be held about how it might be improved or changed. Ask them about what sort of things are in their homes and what they are used for.

You may decide to include a kitchen, bedroom, and sitting room, or focus on one area such as the kitchen. This could be useful if you want to use it within a specific cross-curricular area such as a unit of work on food or to use it in a history unit.

Once you and the class have decided what the area will be like, as with the other activities, begin to put it together.

Resources required – Play furniture such as cookers, sink, cot or cradle, doll's pram/buggy, table and chairs, cooking, eating and drinking utensils, play food, variety of clothes, covers, telephone, paper and pencils (for writing shopping lists, etc.), dolls. Televisions, video and DVD players are heavy with possible hazardous parts so even if you can acquire old ones that no longer work it might be a better idea to make these items out of cardboard boxes, and more fun too.

Cross-curricular links – Literacy, DT, history.

When to do it – In literacy within units of work such as stories with familiar settings and plays.

Design and technology – in a unit of work on food technology.

History – knowledge and understanding of events, people and changes in the past – compare and contrast cooking now with selected periods in the past.

Use of teaching assistants – As previously stated.

NLS and Foundation Stage objectives

Foundation Stage – Communication, language and literacy

Language for communication
Listen to others in one-to-one/small groups when conversation interests them.

Enjoy listening to and using spoken language and readily turn to it in their play and learning.

Interact with others, negotiating plans and activities and taking turns in conversation.

Language for thinking
Use language to imagine and re-create roles and experiences.

Creative development
Engage in imaginative role-play based on own first-hand experiences.

Play alongside other children who are engaged in the same theme.

Play co-operatively as part of a group to act out a narrative.

Year 1 Term 1

Text level
T7 To re-enact stories in a variety of ways, e.g. through role-play, using dolls or puppets.

Year 1 Term 2
T9 To become aware of character and dialogue, e.g. by role-playing parts when reading aloud stories or plays with others.

Year 2 Term 2

Text level
T7 To prepare and re-tell stories individually and through role-play in groups, using dialogue and narrative from text.

PNS objectives – Speaking, listening and learning
Year 1 Term 1

4. Drama
To explore familiar themes and characters through improvisation and role-play, e.g. using story boxes and bags of props to create characters.

Link with NLS text objective 7.

Year 1 Term 2

8. Drama

To act out own and well-known stories, using different voices for characters e.g. using drama techniques to portray characters, and motives.

Link with NLS text objectives 9 and 15.

Year 2 Term 3

24. Drama

To present parts of traditional stories, own stories or work from different parts of the curriculum for members of their class, e.g. deciding which parts of a story to dramatise and developing a polished presentation of a key moment.

Further comments and suggestions – Home-corner equipment can be turned quite effectively into settings for traditional stories, such as the Three Bears' cottage, Grandmother's cottage, or the Gingerbread cottage from 'Hansel and Gretel'. Children can be given time for free play in these area or they can be used in a more structured way in literacy, linking with the NLS focus of traditional stories.

Talk in the curriculum – talk areas

Children's conversation during their school day could be considered an activity in itself that helps language development. It can be interesting to discover how many different kinds of talk happen in the classroom.

The following task is excellent for showing the diverse nature of language in the classroom. When the children are working relatively independently, walk around the class and make a note of the sort of conversations you can hear. Make a note at other times of the day during different activities, such as when they are changing for PE, getting ready for lunch, or playing. Do this on enough occasions for you to get a wide range of talk contexts and then look at them carefully.

You will find that the children engage in a wide range of different kinds of talk. There will be argumentative discussion, explanatory and supportive discussion when they try to help their friends, questioning, statements, and of course the general 'noise' of the class singing, humming, oo's and ah's, discussing TV, family and friends as they work. This sort of talk is very important, as it is the verbal equivalent of doodling. It allows the brain to work while no cognitive engagement with external thinking is happening. The talk in free-play situations will be different again.

This will help give you an idea of the different contexts for talk in the class. The sort of talk that happens depends on not only the activity, but how it is organised. The implication is that we can promote particular types of talk through planning specific activities. This is really important if we want to encourage and develop a wide range of language skills including subject-specific vocabulary.

With these thoughts in mind I have included a couple of activities that are not talk activities as such but can nevertheless be used to focus on speaking while being based in a set curriculum area.

Activity 4 — Talk while investigating objects and artefacts

Aims — To use appropriate language to describe objects, take turns in speaking, make relevant comments, enhance listening skills, extend ideas in the light of discussion, relate their contribution to what has gone before.

What to do — Ensure children are seated so that they can all see you; seating them in a horseshoe works well if you have the space because you can also see them. Explain that you have some items in a box that you are going to share with them. What you have in the box will depend on the subject being taught.

Open the box slowly, make a big secret and a game out of it and produce an item from the box for the children to discuss. Use open questioning to get the children to really think about the item and to discuss it fully.

Resources required — Box, items to go in it. This will depend on the subject matter (see Further comments and suggestions).

Cross-curricular links — All subjects that have specific items that can be associated with them, such as music (musical instruments), science (depending on the topic, magnets, torches, batteries, wire, etc.), design and technology (staplers, hole punches, different scissors,) history (artefacts to do with a topic, e.g. toys, homes in the past, the Victorians, the Second World War, etc.).

When to do it — As part of any lesson but particularly as an introduction to a topic or at the beginning of a particular lesson that has a specific focus. In the Foundation Stage an activity such as this might come under the 'knowledge and understanding of the world' area of learning.

Use of teaching assistants — Ensure children are focused, support individuals and selected groups, offer prompts and suggestions.

NLS and Foundation Stage objectives
Foundation Stage — Communication, language and literacy
Language for communication
Listen to others in one-to-one/small groups when conversation interests them.

Enjoy listening to and using spoken language and readily turn to it in their play and learning.

Interact with others, negotiating plans and activities and taking turns in conversation.

PNS objectives – Speaking, listening and learning

Year 1 Term 2

7. Group discussion and interaction
To take turns to speak, listen to others' suggestions and talk about what they are going to do, e.g. devising simple rules for turn-taking and contributing in groups.

Year 2 Term 2

19. Group discussion and interaction
To ensure everyone contributes, allocate tasks, consider alternatives and reach agreement, e.g. working collaboratively in planning, predicting and carrying out an investigative task.

Further comments and suggestions – There are lots of ways of adapting and using this activity. I first tried it when working with a class of Year 2 children. As part of a history lesson we were looking at changes in how we live and I had borrowed a box of artefacts from the local museum to try to get the point across. Before I had even opened the box the children were trying to guess what was in it and couldn't wait for it to be opened!

The children had to guess what the items had been used for, and if possible say why they thought so. For example, one item was a toasting fork; they guessed it was for eating because it looked a bit like a dinner fork but couldn't work out why it had such a long handle.

A great deal of discussion arose from this activity and the children learnt a lot about changes in the home over the years. This was just as well as I had an Ofsted inspector in the class at the time! I was really pleased when he rated the lesson very good and this was a lesson based completely around talk and discussion.

Other ideas might be in science to introduce the equipment related to a topic or music to discuss a range of less familiar instruments. The discussion in this case might be about what sound the instrument will make and to guess how you would play it.

Activity 5 – Talk while investigating materials

Aims – To use appropriate language to describe objects, take turns in speaking, make relevant comments, enhance listening skills, extend ideas in the light of discussion, relate their contribution to what has gone before.

What to do – I did this in an art lesson but the same could be done in any lesson involving investigation such as science or maths. We were investigating a variety of materials closely, using magnifying glasses to look at texture, colour, pattern, etc. Prior to this we had looked at the properties of different materials, seeing how they folded, pleated, and whether they could be cut or torn.

Set up the activity by placing a variety of different materials on each table. The children can then select a piece of material to work with. On one table (more if you have the resources) place a tape recorder.

Deliver your lesson and send the children to the tables to begin work. At first go to groups and listen to what they are saying without participating yourself. This is always difficult with young children because they are so keen to share their experiences with you. After a while sit with selected groups and ask them about their work. Encourage them to explain what they have found out. This is a good activity in which to use open questioning to get children to give answers that require some thought, using sentences rather than one-word answers.

You can decide how to use the tape recorder. You might want to start it when you join the group to talk about their work or you could leave it to run for the course of the session so that you get a contrast between conversations happening when the children were working independently and when they were talking with you.

Resources required – Audiotapes, tape recorder, whatever items you require for the lesson being taught. The lesson I used needed a variety of materials, e.g. cloth such as wool, cotton (lace is a nice one because of the intricate patterns), synthetic material, mixed fibres, plastic, different papers and cardboards; also magnifying glasses, paper for recording, drawing and colouring pencils.

Cross-curricular links – Any subject where children are involved in investigation such as science, maths, design and technology, music, history, geography. The activity can be adapted and organised to suit subject and learning intentions. Areas of learning of the Foundation Stage that might include this activity are 'knowledge and understanding of the world' and 'creative development'.

When to do it – Within a lesson as an investigative activity following teaching input.

Use of teaching assistants – Talk to children and help to keep them focused, support groups and individuals, reinforce learning intentions. If confident and resources allow, use the tape recorder in the same way as the teacher.

NLS and Foundation Stage objectives

Foundation Stage – Communication, language and literacy

Language for communication
Use their senses to explore and investigate objects – begin to recognise/talk about similarities and differences.

Listen to others in one-to-one/small groups when conversation interests them.

Enjoy listening to and using spoken language and readily turn to it in their play and learning.

Interact with others, negotiating plans and activities and taking turns in conversation.

> ## PNS objectives – Speaking, listening and learning
>
> ### Year 1 Term 2
>
> *7. Group discussion and interaction*
> To take turns to speak, listen to others' suggestions and talk about what they are going to do, e.g. devising simple rules for turn-taking and contributing in groups.
>
> ### Year 2 Term 2
>
> *19. Group discussion and interaction*
> To ensure everyone contributes, allocate tasks, consider alternatives and reach agreement, e.g. working collaboratively in planning, predicting and carrying out an investigative task.

Further comments and suggestions – When I did this activity the children were drawing what they were looking at, which meant they were thinking carefully about their observations and were processing their findings visually and orally. Drawing combined with discussion seemed to help the thought process, a little like the verbal doodling referred to earlier.

You do not have to use a tape recorder: the children will make their comments regardless but it is useful to play back the children's comments so you can listen to them more carefully. Listening to the tapes afterwards can be time consuming but it is surprising what you miss in the general hubbub of classroom chat. The children's comments can be quite enlightening. I was able to determine from listening to transcripts of my recordings how important the act of talking was for the children to check their thoughts and ideas. They would not have learnt as much and made the progress they did without the interactive dialogue that occurred.

These 'talk areas' in the classroom can have the problem that it is difficult to hear and decipher what the children are saying, particularly those who are not closest to the microphone, above the general noise of the classroom. As the whole purpose of these sorts of activities is to encourage talk while investigating or working, it would defeat the object to tell the children to work silently. One solution is to remind the rest of the class that you are recording and ask them to try to keep the general noise level down, such as the scraping of chairs. Children can be surprisingly co-operative when they think they might be on the tape.

As already mentioned in previous activities, make sure the children are clear about your expectations and know exactly how they are to behave with the recorders, bearing in mind health and safety issues. They will become used to having them in the class and will understand what you expect, the more you use them.

A talk corner

Most classrooms have reading corners and some might have writing corners – but what about talk corners? A talk corner can include a discussion box where children put ideas that they would like to talk about, telephones with the 'numbers' of familiar story-book characters to ring up, tape machines and blank tapes, dictaphones, tape players and story and song tapes including stories in community languages, plus headphones.

It will depend on your classroom how easy or difficult this is to set up. Children need to be clear about the ground rules for using a talk corner and it may need discussion in the same way as rules for behaviour are discussed to establish this.

The problem of noise might arise if recording is to take place. Arrangements for taping might have to be during a quiet time in the class. Alternatively it might be possible to arrange with the whole staff an area that could be designated as a recording studio that is relatively quiet. A booking system would have to be put into place and children could go in pairs or small groups to record plays and other extended spoken texts. This particular idea is probably suited to older children, although a good use of teaching assistants would be to support all children in this area.

Drama, role-play and mime

This chapter includes:
The use of selected drama activities including hot-seating and paired improvisation in:

- Literacy
- PE
- Art
- History.

Drama and role-play are brilliant tools for learning and they fit quite easily into literacy and other subjects across the curriculum. I have included here some of the activities that have worked well for me.

Issues of self-confidence

Being in role can be worrying for some individuals, child and adult alike, and can require a certain amount of confidence. If you are one of the less confident sort, try not to be self-conscious; the children love watching teachers and other adults in role, and you most certainly do not lose any dignity or respect. Not all children are natural actors either; some may be reluctant to have a go at certain activities so you need to be aware of this and treat incidents sensitively.

In the next activity the children have to work out who the traditional story character is through discussion and questioning.

Activity 1 – Guess the traditional or fairy story character

Aims – To encourage participation, choose words with precision, organise what they say, include relevant detail, ask questions to clarify their understanding, sustain concentration, take turns in speaking, relate their contributions to what has gone before.

What to do – Explain to the children that they are going to try to guess a traditional story character. Model the activity first to give the children a good idea of what you want them to do. Choose a well-known character to start with, such as Red Riding Hood, and ask the children to work out your character by asking questions.

At first you will probably find they start by naming lots of characters at random. You will need to remind them that to work out your character they need to ask questions to determine who you are. Some examples might be: 'Are you a male or female character?' 'Are you a human?' 'Are you good or a bad character?'

The best way to help them get the idea is to model it with a willing adult who can ask the sorts of questions the children need to ask. This also allows the children to hear the answers you give.

When they seem to have got the idea, choose a child to have a go. At this stage decide on someone who you know is quite articulate and will be able to answer questions accurately. Allow the child to sit in your chair as this gives them a sense of importance!

Some children know exactly which character they are going to be while others will need some support. You can use the pack of character cards to help if you wish (see photocopiables on page 33–5) These can help a child to decide who to be and also prevent cheating. Children love being the character so much that some of them will try to stay there by not admitting when their character has been guessed!

Give the child the character cards to choose from. The child then removes the card and places it where no one else can see it. When their character has been guessed they hold up the card to confirm it. Of course some children will know who they want to be without the cards, in which case they can whisper to you who they are.

At first you may have to guide the questioning and remind the children of the sorts of questions to ask. You might also have to help the child in role with their answers. Be aware that some children will always need support and may find the activity difficult. Don't exclude them from having the opportunity to sit on the hot-seat but offer to help them by suggesting a character and prompting them if they are stuck with the answer or do not understand the question. The boost to their self-esteem from this can be enormous.

Encourage the rest of the class to work together to discuss who the character is by reminding themselves about traditional story characters and which questions have been asked.

When the routine is established, this can be used as an independent activity for the children to work at in pairs.

Resources required – A teacher's chair, pictures of traditional and fairy-story characters (helpful but not essential).

Cross-curricular links – Literacy.

When to do it – During the literacy hour within a unit of work on fairy stories or traditional stories, as well as characters from other genres who can be guessed in the same way, for instance Shirley Hughes's 'Alfie'.

Use of teaching assistants – To offer support to less confident children with prompts and suggestions, act as partner for the teacher when modelling the activity, take a turn in role themselves to help reinforce teaching input, support pairs of children during independent work.

NLS and Foundation Stage objectives

Foundation Stage – Communication, language and literacy

Language for communication
Begin to use more complex sentences.

Use language for an increasing range of purposes.

Sustain attentive listening, responding to what they have heard by relevant comments, questions or actions.

Language for thinking
Begin to use talk to pretend imaginary situations.

Use language to imagine and recreate roles and experiences.

Year 1 Term 2
T8 To identify and discuss characters, e.g. appearance, behaviour, qualities; to speculate about how they might behave; to discuss how they are described in the text; and to compare characters from different stories or plays.

Further comments and suggestions – I have found this activity works really well in helping children to become familiar with characters from traditional stories. It is particularly useful when children are not that familiar with the genre.

Although questions like those mentioned seem to require one-word answers, in fact the answer is not always cut and dried and children have to think quite hard about how to reply to them. Was Red Riding Hood good or bad? Generally we think of her as good because she helped her mother, but some of the children I have worked with are quite firm in their belief that she was naughty because she should not have talked to a stranger! This of course is a good topic for debate, which I discuss in another section.

Hot-seating

Hot-seating is a drama strategy that involves an individual to go into role as a character, either fictional or historical. The chosen child sits in the 'hot-seat' and is questioned as their character about their actions. Hot-seating helps children to focus on a character's motivations, feelings and reasons for their behaviour. The children obviously need to be

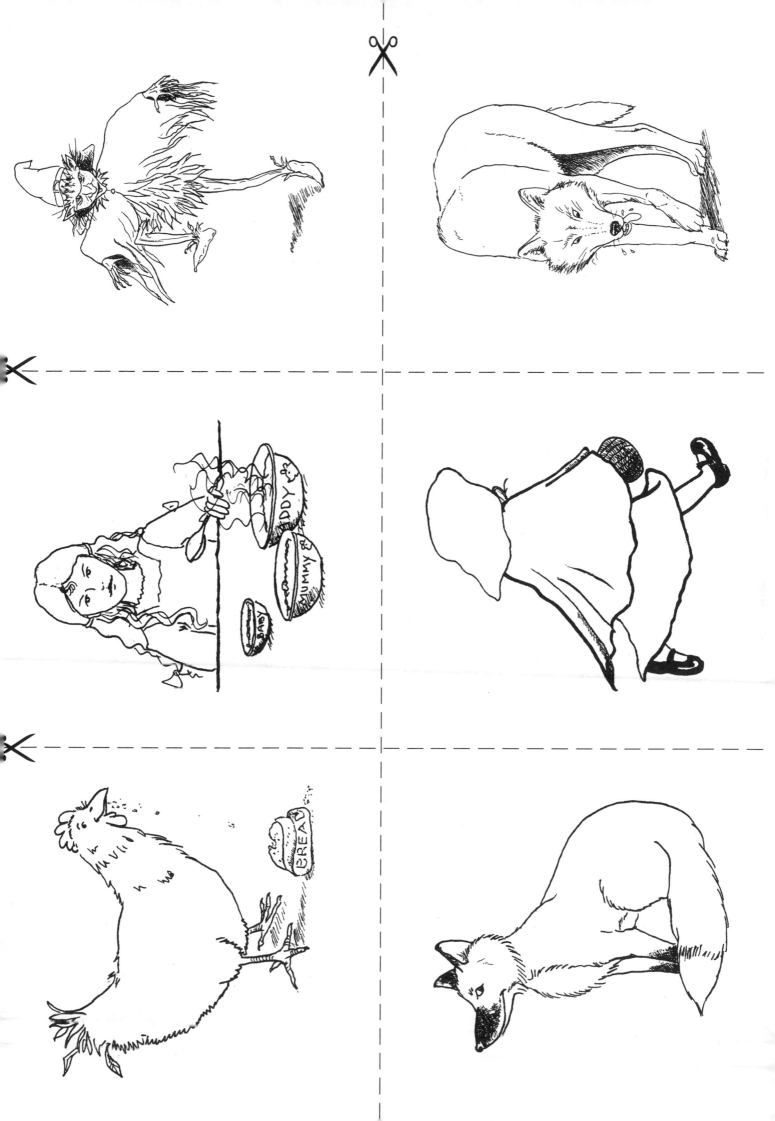

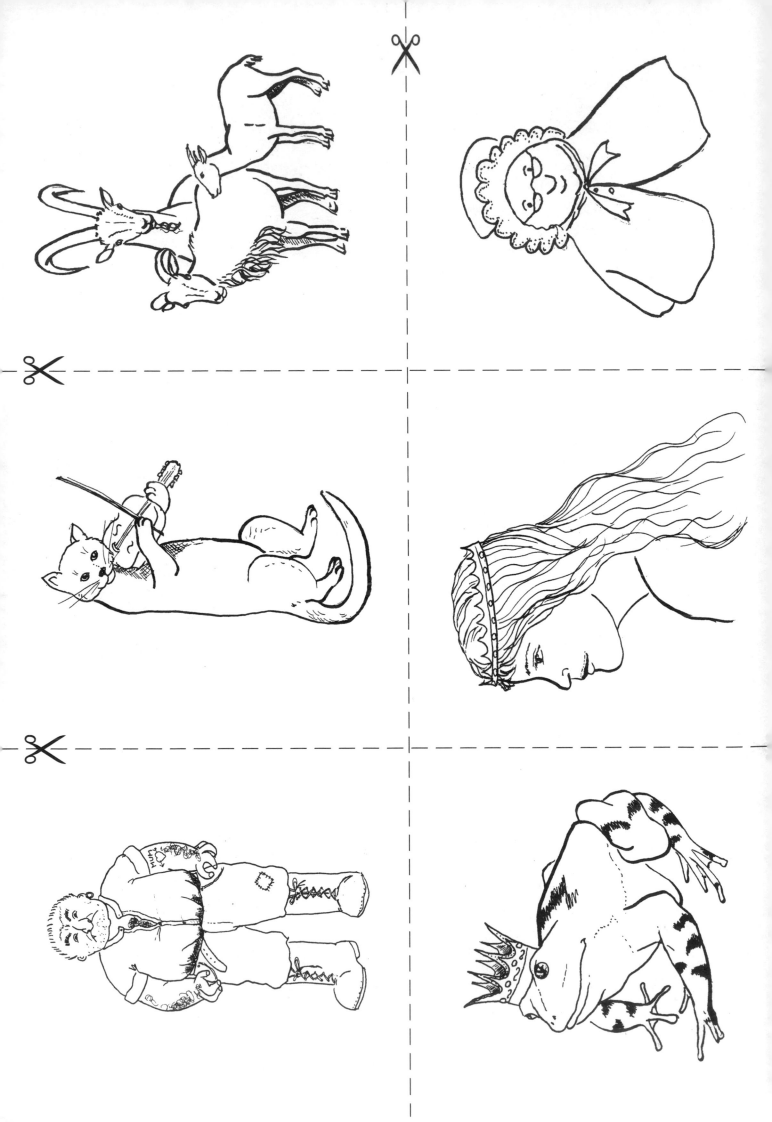

familiar with the character in order for this to work well. I have used it with both fictional characters and figures from history.

The activity that follows was done with a Year 1 class as part of a history lesson. In this particular case the adult was in role but children can take on a role very well and soon get the idea. As always there are those who struggle due to lack of experience and vocabulary and their needs must be considered and appropriate support provided.

Activity 2 – Historical character in the hot-seat

Aims – To encourage participation, choose words with precision, organise what they say, include relevant detail, ask questions to clarify their understanding, sustain concentration, take turns in speaking, relate their contributions to what has gone before, give reasons for opinions and actions.

What to do – Choose an historical figure related to the unit of work being covered. Explain to the children that they will be 'meeting' this character and can ask them questions about their life.

The activity can be organised in various ways. You can be in role from the start, or make sure the children are ready and then go out of the classroom and come back in role. You may decide to tell the children that you are going to pretend to be a character and get ready in front of them.

Use some props, as they are helpful in establishing the character. These do not have to be elaborate; for example, as Guy Fawkes you could wear a wide brimmed floppy hat, stick-on moustache, and perhaps a jacket or long coat. Carry a lantern to add to the effect and the children's imaginations will do the rest, especially if they have watched a video about the Gunpowder Plot. Giving props is also a good way of motivating more reluctant individuals.

It is an idea to have talked to the children about the sorts of things they might ask an historical figure if they were to meet one today. Preparing them in this way will help get the session rolling and also help the children to think about what they want to find out and the sorts of questions they may need to ask.

Sit in the hot-seat and let the questions begin. The way the session goes after this depends very much on the questions, your answers and the children's reactions to them.

Resources required – A few props to match whatever character is in the hot-seat; a suggestion of the character is all that is needed.

Cross-curricular links – History.

When to do it – In history to help focus on historical figures such as Florence Nightingale, Guy Fawkes or other significant historical figures such as Henry VIII at Key Stage 2. In the Foundation Stage an activity such as this might come under the 'knowledge and understanding of the world' area of learning. In literacy during a unit of work on traditional characters, fairy stories, myths and legends or any character whose actions can be questioned.

Use of teaching assistants – To watch the class if you choose to go out to get into role, support children and remind them of what they could ask, monitor behaviour and keep children focused, support with questioning.

NLS and Foundation Stage objectives

Foundation Stage – Communication, language and literacy

Language for communication
Begin to use more complex sentences.

Use language for an increasing range of purposes.

Sustain attentive listening, responding to what they have heard by relevant comments, questions or actions.

Language for thinking
Begin to use talk to pretend imaginary situations.

Use language to imagine and recreate roles and experiences.

Year 1 Term 2

T8 To identify and discuss characters, e.g. appearance, behaviour, qualities; to speculate about how they might behave; to discuss how they are described in the text; and to compare characters from different stories or plays.

Year 2 Term 2

T6 To identify and describe characters, expressing own views and using words and phrases from texts.

Year 3 Term 3

T5 To discuss (i) characters' feelings; (ii) behaviour, e.g. fair or unreasonable, brave or foolish; (iii) relationships, referring to the text and making judgements.

Further comments and suggestions – It is interesting to note with young children how ready they are to believe in you as the character. They will watch you get changed in front of them and still think you are actually that character. This can be helpful if you are self-conscious about going into role. Children are very willing to believe in you however silly you may feel and the questions and discussions that can be generated, I think, are well worth being brave and having a try.

It is also worth making sure that you are reasonably knowledgeable about your character if it is an historical one, as some bright spark will always think of a question you may not have anticipated.

Some other examples of characters for the hot-seat are, the Big Bad Wolf, Goldilocks and the giant from traditional stories and, at Key Stage 2, characters from the Greek myths.

Paired improvisation

I first did this with a Year 1 class as part of work we were doing in the literacy hour on traditional stories. As well as letting them re-enact the stories in the role-play area I thought it would be a different way of looking at the characters, and one they had not done before. This technique involves children been given roles, and then making up a dialogue in pairs between their characters. This strategy helps get the children into role and also makes them really think about the characters they have chosen. Characters from the same story can be chosen, but the children tend to stick with the dialogue they know from the stories, without extending it. Using characters from two different stories, such as Red Riding Hood and Goldilocks, means they really have to think of their characters and make up an appropriate conversation.

Activity 3 – What did one character say to the other?

Aims – To encourage participation, enhance listening skills, respond appropriately, take turns in speaking, speak with clear diction and appropriate intonation, choose words with precision, take into account the needs of their listeners, listen to others' reactions, take turns in speaking, relate their contributions to what has gone before, create and sustain roles individually and when working with others.

What to do – As usual, explain to the children what you are all going to be doing. The best way to explain this is to model it, providing you have a willing grown-up with you. If this is not possible, choose two confident, articulate speakers from the class and talk them through it in front of the class.

Choose the characters for them, for example, Jack and Red Riding Hood. Get each child to think about their character, what they are like, how they behaved in the story, etc. and then share it with the class. The other children can help with suggestions if they get stuck.

Next, prompt them as to the sorts of things the characters might say with questions like: 'What do two people say when they meet for the first time?' 'Where are the characters going?' 'Will Red Riding Hood tell Jack about the wolf, or has that part of the story not happened yet?' These are the sorts of questions the children will need to consider when going into role.

The conversation may go something like this.

Hello, my name is Red Riding Hood, who are you?
I'm Jack, and this is my cow, Milky White.
Where are you going with her?
Well, see, my mum says we've got to sell her and I'm taking her to the market.
Yeah, I know, have you noticed how Mums are always telling you to do stuff? My Mum is always getting me to go visit my Grandma. It's dead boring! Nothin' exciting ever happens . . .

The sort of conversation you get will depend on the age of the children, the cohort (some children are more articulate than others), and their experience of this sort of activity.

Younger children, and those without a great deal of experience of stories and narrative, may well find it hard to expand the dialogue beyond the very simple. The more opportunities they are given to try this and the more examples they see, the better they will become.

When you feel the children have got the idea, send them off in pairs to have a go. You will have to decide whether to tell them which characters to be or to let them choose for themselves.

Move about the class listening to the children's conversations. Offer support and suggestions if the children are really stuck but try to ensure that the children work things out for themselves as much as possible. Make a mental note of any really good conversations, and children who co-operated well by listening to each other.

At the end of the session bring the class together and seat them in a horseshoe. Ask them to remind you what they have been doing and why and mention some children who worked well. At this point you could ask any of the children if they would like to share their work with the rest of the class. Most children are keen to do this but I never insist that they have to do it. They can then sit in the gap of the horseshoe to show what they did. This is a good opportunity for the rest of the class to see how their peers worked. It should be more than a 'show and tell'. Use it to reinforce the technique, and point out what worked particularly well. The rest of the class can contribute by commenting on the dialogues and saying what they thought was good and why. Try to encourage positive comments – but this does not mean suggestions of how it might be even better can't be made. It is not what is said but how it's said.

Resources required – None.

Cross-curricular links – History, literacy.

When to do it – During the literacy hour, as part of a history lesson.

Use of teaching assistants – To help model activity when it is being introduced, to monitor and support children in their pairs, work with selected pairs of children requiring extra support, ensure class are focused and support individuals in the whole-class sessions.

NLS and Foundation Stage objectives

Foundation Stage – Communication, language and literacy

Language for communication
Use language for an increasing range of purposes.

Sustain attentive listening, responding to what they have heard by relevant comments, questions or actions.

Enjoy listening to and using spoken written language, and readily turn to it in their play and learning.

Consistently develop a simple story, explanation or line of questioning.

Language for thinking
Use talk to pretend imaginary situations.

Use language to imagine and recreate roles and experiences.

Year 1 Term 2
T8 To identify and discuss characters, e.g. appearance, behaviour, qualities; to speculate about how they might behave; to discuss how they are described in the text; and to compare characters from different stories or plays.

T9 To become aware of character and dialogue, e.g. by role-playing parts when reading aloud stories or plays with others.

PNS objectives – Speaking, listening and learning
Year 3 Term 1

28. Drama
To present events and characters through dialogue to engage the interest of an audience, e.g. acting out a dialogue between two characters, bringing out the differences between them.

Link with NLS text objectives 2 and 3.

Further comments and suggestions – This activity can be quite challenging for some children; however, with support in time it is surprising what can be achieved.

Likewise, if you find it challenging, don't give up. The results from the children are well worth it. I have had some wonderful dialogues from children. One pair of children, an extremely articulate girl and an inarticulate boy, worked brilliantly together and made up an excellent conversation. The boost to the boy's self-esteem was amazing.

Mime and other drama activities

Of course, not all drama activities require speaking. Mime might seem less daunting to those children who are not so confident. You are probably wondering how mime can encourage speaking, as that is the one thing it does not involve. I have worked with children in Years 1, 2 and 3 using the following activity and have had some excellent speaking and discussion arising from it.

Short activities to introduce mime
I have used mime in a variety of contexts, including PE, with some great results. If the children have had no experience of mime I have found it is best to explain what it is and then, as usual, model it. Choose to mime something that the children will be familiar with so that they can immediately relate to it and see what you are doing, such as answering the telephone, using a skipping rope or bouncing a ball. Let the children

experiment with some ideas. Explain that in mime, movements and expressions need to be exaggerated to compensate for the lack of speech.

Pick out some good examples to show the class. Let the children try to guess the mimes and say what it was in the mime that helped them. When the children seem to have got the idea, have a go at the next activity.

Activity 4 – Secret mimes

Aims – Encourage participation, sustain concentration, make relevant comments, take turns in speaking, create and sustain roles individually and when working with others, comment constructively on drama they have watched or in which they have taken part.

What to do – Put the children into small groups. How you do this will depend on your class; you may let the children choose their friends or decide to sort them yourself with behaviour and ability in mind.

Before the lesson write on some cards a mime for the children to perform. An example might be 'Going shopping', 'Having a picnic' or 'Going swimming'. Explain to the children that they are going to be given a secret mime for their groups to act and everyone else to guess. Emphasise the secret nature of the game and that they must not let their classmates know what is on their card. This adds to the fun.

Give a card to each group and tell them they must work out the mime on the card. They must co-operate to decide who will do what. You may have to use a picture rather than writing with very young children or those with reading difficulties. Placing a competent reader in each group to read the cards is another idea.

Allow the children time to work out and practise their mime. You will need to circulate around the groups to support them and possibly to sort out arguments. When you think they have had long enough and most are ready, stop them and begin to show the mimes.

Get the children watching to put up their hands when they think they know the mime and to say how they guessed it. They need to explain how they guessed.

Resources required – Cards with mime activities written or drawn on them.

Cross-curricular links – Literacy, history, PE.

When to do it – As part of a literacy lesson in a unit of work on traditional stories or fairy stories, in PE to show how to use a piece of equipment, in a history lesson to reinforce a particular event or incident.

Use of teaching assistants – To support groups of children in working out their mime.

NLS and Foundation Stage objectives
Foundation Stage – Communication, language and literacy
Language for communication
Begin to use more complex sentences.

Use talk to comment on ideas, explain what is happening (and anticipate what might happen next).

Use talk to organise, sequence and clarify thinking, ideas, feelings and events.

Use language for an increasing range of purposes.

Sustain attentive listening, responding to what they have heard (in this case seen) by relevant comments, questions or actions.

Creative development

Engage in imaginative role-play based on own first-hand experience.

Play co-operatively as part of a group to act out a narrative.

PNS objectives – Speaking, listening and learning

Year 1 Term 2

7. Group discussion and interaction
To take turns to speak, listen to others' suggestions and talk about what they are going to do, e.g. devising simple rules for turn-taking and contributing in groups.

Year 2 Term 1

15. Group discussion and interaction
To listen to each other's views and preferences, agree the next steps to take and identify contributions by each group member, e.g. learning how to pool views, make decisions and allocate tasks.

Year 2 Term 2

19. Group discussion
To ensure everyone contributes, allocate tasks, consider alternatives and reach agreement, e.g. working collaboratively in planning, predicting and carrying out an investigative task.

Year 3 Term 2

31. Group discussion and interaction
To actively include and respond to all members of the group, e.g. encouraging contributions by use of questions, eye contact and people's names when discussing an issue.

Further comments and suggestions – Providing cards with ideas for mime helps prevent time being wasted while the children struggle to think of and agree on a mime of their own. Cards are also useful if you are using this activity in a particular lesson within a specific subject, e.g. older children learning about the Ancient Greeks could try miming an incident from different myths written on cards.

This is also a nice activity to use as part of literacy by getting children to mime a traditional story and for the others to guess it.

I usually make a big thing of the 'performance' so that the children feel really important and know that their contribution is valued. Get some benches out if you are working in the hall so that the 'audience' have somewhere to sit, and remind them about acceptable behaviour, i.e. not making fun of their classmates.

This next activity is a drama activity that involves the whole class. It is a great activity for children who lack confidence because they are included with everyone and supported by the whole class. The idea came from a drama INSET held a number of years ago at the school where I was teaching. A visiting drama specialist worked with the staff to show how drama and role-play can be used across the curriculum.

Activity 5 – The Three Billy Goats Gruff

Aims – Speak with clear diction and appropriate intonation, sustain concentration, take turns in speaking, use language and actions to explore and convey situations, characters and emotions, encourage participation for all, work co-operatively.

What to do – You will need a large space to do this activity as it involves the whole class. The hall is ideal but failing this, depending on individual circumstances, furniture in the classroom can be moved to make a space.

Explain to the children they are all going to act out the story of 'The Three Billy Goats Gruff'. You will need some children to play the troll and the goats. The rest of the class will be the bridge. After you have decided on your four main players, divide the rest of the class into two.

Get the children to stand in two lines facing each other approximately one metre apart. This forms the bridge, and the troll and goats walk in between the lines of children, as they cross the bridge to act out the story. The children forming the bridge need to listen carefully because as the 'goats' walk over it (through the lines of children) they make the noise of the bridge. If the children link their arms it helps them to stay together and for the bridge not to 'drift apart'. There are lots of different versions of this story. The one I know best, reads: 'Trip, Trap! Trip, Trap! Trip, Trap! went the rickety, rackety, wooden bridge.'

As the goats cross the bridge, the children say 'trip, trap, trip, trap, trip, trap', getting progressively louder with each goat to indicate the size of the goats. They could also add a creaking and groaning sound for effect. The children can sway slightly to help suggest the bridge moving as it is crossed.

As the children get the idea, depending on time you can swap your goats and troll with some of those who are making up the bridge. This allows others to have a turn.

Resources required – None required for the actual activity, but props such as masks can be used.

Cross-curricular links – PE, music, literacy.

When to do it – In PE as part of work involving music and movement, in music covering POS 1, 3, and 4 at Key Stage 1. In literacy as part of a unit of work on traditional stories.

Use of teaching assistants – To help organise the class as the teacher directs, monitor behaviour, support individuals.

NLS and Foundation Stage objectives

Foundation Stage – Communication, language and literacy

Language for communication
Begin to use more complex sentences.

Use language for an increasing range of purposes.

Sustain attentive listening, responding to what they have heard by relevant comments, questions or actions.

Enjoy listening to and using spoken written language, and readily turn to it in their play and learning.

Creative development
Imaginative role-play based on own first-hand experience.

Play co-operatively as part of a group to act out a narrative.

Year 1 Term 1
T7 To re-enact stories in a variety of ways, e.g. through role-play, using dolls or puppets.

Year 1 Term 2
T9 To become aware of character and dialogue, e.g. by role-playing parts when reading aloud stories or plays with others.

Year 1 Term 3
T5 To re-tell stories, to give the main points in sequence and to pick out significant incidents.

Further comments and suggestions – This is a great activity for total inclusion; no one needs to be left out or feel worried about doing it, which is great for SEN children and those who lack confidence. It also has the potential to be adapted to other stories, for example 'Red Riding Hood'.

For this you need your main characters, and the rest of the class become the wood. You can decide what sound effects to use, such as the rustling of leaves or perhaps the padding of wolf paws and panting of his breath. The children need to be standing in a group, placed as trees in a wood. To emulate paws, try getting them to pat their thighs gently in a rhythm that suggests a prowling wolf.

Another enactment that works well using the whole class is based on the well-known rhyme 'We're Going on a Bear Hunt'.

Activity 6 – We're Going on a Bear Hunt

Aims – Speak with clear diction and appropriate intonation, sustain concentration, take turns in speaking, use language and actions to explore and convey situations, characters and emotions, encourage participation for all, work co-operatively.

What to do – This activity needs to be done after the children have become familiar with the rhyme. In Year 1 I use Michael Rosen and Helen Oxenbury's lovely version of this story as a text in the literacy hour. I usually find that the children are already familiar with it from the early years but if not this is a great book to use.

Once the children know it, explain that you are all going to act it out. Choose someone to be the 'bear', the rest of the class are the other characters.

You will need to be in quite a large space for this such as the hall or playground. Set up the 'bear' in his or her cave (a small tent will do nicely). The rest of the class start from 'home' and recite the rhyme as they move slowly towards the 'cave'. You can denote 'home' either by any markings there might be on the playground, or by using PE mats in the hall.

   You will need to lead the hunt to make sure the children do not get to the 'cave' too fast. Have a rule that they all need to stay behind you. When everyone gets to the 'cave' the bear has to come out of his or her cave and chase you all back the way you came until the class are back 'home' and say 'We're not going on a bear hunt again!'

   If there is time, repeat the activity with a different bear. You will get fed up of repeating it long before the children do!

Resources required – Small tent (this could be a children's play tent or house), mask or similar prop for the bear (neither of these resources is essential in order to do the activity but they do make it more fun).

Cross-curricular links – Literacy, music, PE.

When to do it – In PE in dance activities, literacy in a unit of work on 'stories and rhymes with predictable patterns', music within 'controlling sounds through singing and playing–performing skills'.

Use of teaching assistants – To help organise the class as teacher directs, monitor behaviour, support individuals and groups.

NLS and Foundation Stage objectives

Foundation Stage – Communication, language and literacy

Language for communication
Listen to favourite nursery rhymes, stories and songs. Join in with repeated refrains, anticipating key events and important phrases.

Enjoy listening to and using spoken written language, and readily turn to it in their play and learning.

Creative development

Imaginative role-play based on own first-hand experience.

Play co-operatively as part of a group to act out a narrative.

Year 1 Term 1

Text Level

T7 To re-enact stories in a variety of ways, e.g. through role-play, using dolls or puppets.

Year 1 Term 2

Text Level

T9 To become aware of character and dialogue, e.g. by role-playing parts when reading aloud stories or plays with others.

Year 1 Term 3

Text level

T5 To re-tell stories, to give the main points in sequence and to pick out significant incidents.

Further comments and suggestions – Children love this activity and can get somewhat excited, especially when the bear chases them. You will need to be quite firm about behaviour. One way of reminding them is to say you are looking for someone really sensible to be the bear next time and they must show you how good they can be. This activity is particularly good for younger children.

Story boxes, story bags and story telling

This chapter includes:

- Ways of story telling including the use of props

- Re-telling stories

- Comparing stories

- Using talk boxes or tins.

Children can find it very difficult to re-tell stories and even harder to make them up. This is particularly so if they have not had much experience of stories and story telling. There is a variety of ways to involve children with texts, and the use of 'story bags' is one that not only can spark an interest in reading but also involves much talk and discussion, which is why I have included it here.

A story bag is a bag containing a book, plus items associated with the story, which might include characters in the form of soft toys or puppets. There might also be a non-fiction book on a similar theme, which allows children to experience different types of text. These items are used to help bring the story to life. They provide a visual and tactile stimulus that the children can use to take part in the telling or re-telling of the story. Children of all abilities enjoy using them but they can be particularly useful in helping children who are not interested in reading, for whatever reasons, to enjoy books. You can make your own story bag and include whatever you feel is appropriate for the children who will be using it.

I was introduced to the idea of story bags about ten or eleven years ago. A member of the learning support team for our area suggested them as a means of engaging children with special needs, particularly those struggling to access basic literacy skills. She presented me with just one bag that her department had made. It contained a copy of *Goldilocks and the Three Bears*, a factual book all about bears, hand puppets of Goldilocks and three different sized bears, plus a soft toy polar bear. The interest and enthusiasm this bag created with children, particularly boys, who before only shared books with reluctance, was amazing.

I used the following activity in the literacy hour within a unit of work on traditional stories. The story was 'Little Red Riding Hood'. This is one way of using this resource that I felt worked for me. You may well have read about or know of different methods and approaches.

Activity 1 – Share a story bag

Aims – To promote discussion, speak with clear diction and appropriate intonation, organise what is said, focus on the main points, include relevant detail, make relevant comments, take turns in speaking, use language to explore and convey situations, characters and emotions.

What to do – Choose a group of children to work with; the size of the group will depend on what you aim to do with them and what the text is. Seat the children around you, either at a table or on the floor depending on your preference and class organisation. Children love guessing and surprises and you can use this as a way of making the activity really exciting.

Ask the children to guess what might be in the bag. They must listen to their friends in the group and try to give reasons for their guess. They often find this quite hard. Next give them a clue by producing a character. Children are usually very familiar with this story and are likely to guess straight away after they have seen a character. However you can still get them to reflect and talk about it and you need not tell them they were right straight away.

Ask them if they still think the story in the bag is 'Red Riding Hood', and then produce another character and continue in this way. Of course they will soon realise they were right the first time but lots of talk and discussion can be done about books, characterisations, stereotypes (depending on the age of the children) and the genre in general.

There are various ways of proceeding. You could ask a volunteer to tell the story while the others listen and see if anything is omitted. You can read the book to them, or if there is a confident reader in the group they might like to read it to their classmates. Most versions of 'Red Riding Hood' are short; and remember you can find your own version to suit your children.

Get the children to use the characters from the bag to re-tell the story. This is where the size of your group can be important because it is nice for all the children to be involved. Your focus for the session may depend on the overall learning intention of the lesson but here are some ideas all good for developing language and speaking skills:

1. Re-tell the story as it is.
2. Re-tell the story and change the ending.
3. Discuss the characters, who do they like best/least and why?
4. Think of other stories with wolves in and discuss their characters, i.e. good or bad.
5. Re-tell the story making the wolf the good character (this will require some thought, discussion and practice).

6. Discuss and identify the differences between written and oral versions of a text.

7. Discuss the differences between the fiction story and a non-fiction text (a book about wolves could be included in the bag).

Resources required – Red Riding Hood story bag containing a copy of the story, puppets or soft toy replicas of the characters in the story. This will depend on your version of the story but in the more traditional versions the characters are usually Red Riding Hood, mother, grandmother, woodcutter and the wolf. In addition your bag could include a factual book about wolves, plus an audiotape of the story.

Cross-curricular links – Literacy.

When to do it – In literacy as a group activity.

Use of teaching assistants – Take a group and work with them in the same way as the teacher, or as directed (some TAs may not feel confident enough to do this).

NLS and Foundation Stage objectives

Foundation Stage – Communication, language and literacy

Language for communication
Begin to use more complex sentences.

Listen to favourite nursery rhymes, stories and songs. Join in with repeated refrains, anticipating key events and important phrases.

Listen to stories with increasing attention and recall.

Describe main story settings, events and principle characters.

Use language for an increasing range of purposes.

Sustain attentive listening, responding to what they have heard by relevant comments, questions or actions.

Enjoy listening to and using spoken written language, and readily turn to it in their play and learning.

Listen to others in one-to-one/small groups when conversation interests them.

Use a widening range of words to express or elaborate ideas.

Interact with others, negotiating plans and activities and taking turns in conversation.

Language for thinking
Talk activities through, reflecting on and modifying what they are doing.

Use talk to connect ideas, explain what is happening and anticipate what might happen next.

Use talk to pretend imaginary situations.

Use language to imagine and re-create roles and experiences.

Suggest how the story might end.

Use talk to organise, sequence and clarify thinking, ideas, feelings and events.

Reading
Re-tell narratives in the correct sequence, drawing on language patterns of stories.

Reception Year

Text level

T4 To notice the difference between spoken and written forms through re-telling known stories; to compare told versions with what the book 'says'.

T5 To understand how book language works and to use some formal elements when re-telling stories, e.g. 'Once there was . . .' 'She lived in a little . . .', 'he replied . . .'

T7 To use knowledge of familiar texts to re-enact or re-tell to others recounting the main points in correct sequence.

T10 To re-read and recite stories and rhymes with predictable and repeated patterns and experiment with similar rhyming patterns.

Year 1 Term 1

Text level

T3 To notice the difference between spoken and written forms through re-telling known stories; compare oral versions with the written text.

T5 To describe story settings and incidents and relate them to own experience and that of others.

T6 To recite stories and rhymes with predictable and repeating patterns, extemporising on patterns orally by substituting words and phrases, extending patterns, inventing patterns and playing with rhyme.

T7 To re-enact stories in a variety of ways, e.g. through role-play, using dolls or puppets.

Year 1 Term 2

Text level

T4 To re-tell stories, giving the main points in sequence and to notice differences between written and spoken forms in re-telling, e.g. by comparing oral versions with the written text; to refer to relevant phrases and sentences.

T5 To identify and record some key features of story language from a range of stories, and to practise reading and using them, e.g. in oral re-tellings.

T7 To discuss reasons for, or causes of, incidents in stories.

T8 To identify and discuss characters, e.g. appearance, behaviour, qualities; to speculate about how they might behave; to discuss how they are described in the text; and to compare characters from different stories or plays.

T9 To become aware of character and dialogue, e.g. by role-playing parts when reading aloud stories or plays with others.

Year 1 Term 3

Text level

T3 To notice the difference between spoken and written forms through re-telling known stories; compare oral versions with the written text.

T5 To re-tell stories, to give the main points in sequence and to pick out significant incidents.

T6 To prepare and re-tell stories orally, identifying and using some of the more formal features of story language.

Year 2 Term 2

Text level

T3 To discuss and compare story themes.

T5 To discuss story settings; to compare differences; to locate key words and phrases in text; to consider how different settings influence events and behaviour.

T6 To identify and describe characters, expressing own views and using words and phrases from texts.

Year 2 Term 2

Sentence level

S1 To read text aloud with intonation and expression appropriate to the grammar and punctuation.

Text level

T7 To prepare and re-tell stories individually and through role-play in groups, using dialogue and narrative from text.

Year 3 Term 1

Text level

T3 To be aware of the different voices in stories using dramatised readings, showing differences between the narrator and different characters used, e.g. puppets to present stories.

Year 3 Term 3

Text level

T5 To discuss (i) characters' feelings; (ii) behaviour, e.g. fair or unreasonable, brave or foolish; (iii) relationships, referring to the text and making judgements.

PNS objectives – Speaking, listening and learning

Year 1 Term 1

4. Drama

To explore familiar themes and characters through improvisation and role-play, e.g. using story boxes and bags of props to create characters.

Link with NLS text objective 7.

Year 1 Term 2

5. Speaking
To re-tell stories, ordering events using story language, e.g. using different techniques to recall and invent well-structured stories.

Link with NLS text objectives 4 and 5.

Year 2 Term 2

17. Speaking
To tell real and imagined stories using the conventions of familiar story language, e.g. including relevant detail, keeping the listeners' interest and sustaining an account.

Link with NLS text objective 7.

Further comments and suggestions – There is a lot of work that can be generated through this activity. You may find there is too much for one session and decide to continue with it on another occasion.

You can make up your own bags to suit your purpose or genre although this can be time consuming, particularly if you have to search around for the items to go in it. You can enlist others to help find or make items to go in it. The bag could then become a whole-school resource. There are commercially produced ones available but these tend to be expensive.

Story telling

In my experience children love to listen to a story, whether it's a reading from a book, an oral re-telling or listening to an anecdote. Family incidents and accidents seem to be popular talking points. These anecdotes, and other story-telling activities, help children to think of ideas, order their words, and begin to gain control over the story-telling process.

Telling a new story or even re-telling a familiar story without a written text to follow is not easy, but it can be really enjoyable and good fun. Whether your story is written down, or made up, it is important to put plenty of expression and action into it. Keep the pace up and use your voice effectively.

Children love humour but I have found they also love scary stories. You will have to use your judgement and knowledge of your class with this. A teacher I know of had a parent accuse her of giving her son nightmares. All she had done was read lots of picture books with monsters in them because that was their topic at the time.

Reading and telling stories to children should be a staple part of any classroom practice and not just classes in Foundation Stage and Key Stage 1.

Re-telling stories

Re-telling stories forms part of the text level work of the Literacy Strategy, particularly in Years 1 and 2 and also at Foundation Stage. However, re-telling a story can be more tricky than reading one, for adults and children alike.

Some children can find it hard, either because they cannot remember the story or they do not have the language skills. Even a really well-known story such as 'Goldilocks and the Three Bears' can present problems, especially with narrative order and cohesion. To form an idea of how difficult it is, try re-telling a well-known story to yourself or a friend.

Use of props such as puppets can help to jog the memory and focus on the order of the story. It is a good idea to use a story with a simple narrative structure to begin with, particularly if you are not confident yourself or your children struggle to re-tell stories.

Activity 2 – Re-tell a familiar story

Aims – Speak with clear diction and appropriate intonation, choose words with precision, organise what they say, focus on the main points, include relevant detail, take into account the needs of their listeners, sustain concentration, take turns in speaking.

What to do – Start with a familiar story such as 'Red Riding Hood'. This story has a simple structure and is not too long. Explain that you are going to re-tell the story and model it using the props. You may want to have practised this beforehand – it will depend on how confident you are. Tell the children that they must be a good audience and listen carefully so that they will then be able to do the same. After you have modelled it, let the children to have a go.

Here are a couple of suggestions how you could organise it.

1. The children work in groups and re-tell the story together. If you are using puppets or other props make sure there are enough for the whole group or arguments are likely to break out. Ensure that each child re-tells part of the story, otherwise you can find one or two dominant individuals take over. This is a good way to work because the children have the support of their peers and less confident children may feel more able to participate.

2. Put children into pairs to support each other as they re-tell the story together. As with the previous suggestion, make sure that both children contribute to the re-telling.

Resources required – Puppets (finger or stick puppets). Drawings are provided on pages 58–60 with which to make some props for Little Red Riding Hood. They can be photocopied, laminated, and then cut out.

Cross-curricular links – History, literacy.

When to do it – During a history lesson to recount events of the past, in the literacy hour.

Use of teaching assistants – Support groups and individuals as directed.

NLS and Foundation Stage objectives

Foundation Stage – Communication, language and literacy

Language for communication
Use intonation, rhythm and phrasing to make their meaning clear to others.

Begin to use more complex sentences.

Describe main story settings, events and principal characters.

Sustain attentive listening, responding to what they have heard by relevant comments, questions or actions.

Enjoy listening to and using spoken written language, and readily turn to it in their play and learning.

Speak clearly and audibly with confidence and control and show awareness of the listener (for example, by their use of conventions such as greetings, 'please' and 'thank you').

Interact with others, negotiating plans and activities and taking turns in conversation.

Begin to use talk, instead of action to rehearse, reorder and reflect on past experience, linking significant events from own experience and from stories, paying attention to sequence and how events lead into one another.

Begin to use talk to pretend imaginary situations.

Suggest how the story might end.

Use talk to organise, sequence and clarify thinking, ideas, feelings and events.

Reading
Re-tell narratives in the correct sequence, drawing on language patterns of stories.

Reception Year

Text level
T4 To notice the difference between spoken and written forms through re-telling known stories; to compare told versions with what the book 'says'.

T5 To understand how book language works and to use some formal elements when re-telling stories, e.g. 'Once there was . . .', 'She lived in a little . . .', 'he replied . . .'.

T7 To use knowledge of familiar texts to re-enact or re-tell to others recounting the main points in correct sequence.

T10 To re-read and recite stories and rhymes with predictable and repeated patterns and experiment with similar rhyming patterns.

Year 1 Term 2

Text level
T4 To re-tell stories, giving the main points in sequence and to notice differences between written and spoken forms in re-telling, e.g. by comparing oral versions with the written text; to refer to relevant phrases and sentences.

T5 To identify and record some key features of story language from a range of stories, and to practise reading and using them, e.g. in oral re-tellings.

Year 1 Term 3

Text level

T5 To re-tell stories, to give the main points in sequence and to pick out significant incidents.

T6 To prepare and re-tell stories orally, identifying and using some of the more formal features of story language.

Year 2 Term 1

Text level

T3 To be aware of the difference between spoken and written language through comparing oral recounts with text; make use of formal story elements in re-telling.

Year 2 Term 2

Text level

T7 To prepare and re-tell stories individually and through role-play in groups, using dialogue and narrative from text.

PNS objectives – Speaking, listening and learning

Year 1 Term 2

5. Speaking

To re-tell stories, ordering events using story language, e.g. using different techniques to recall and invent well-structured stories.

Link with NLS text objectives 4 and 5.

Year 2 Term 2

17. Speaking

To tell real and imagined stories using the conventions of familiar story language, e.g. including relevant detail, keeping the listeners' interest and sustaining an account.

Link with NLS text objective 7.

Further comments and suggestions – Re-telling stories verbally helps children understand some of the features of narrative such as story structure, settings, and the sequence of events. It provides a situation where they have to think of appropriate words and say them in a clear, structured way. This process can be an introduction to talk for writing.

The next activity is really a development from the last and, like the last, is part of the requirements of the National Literacy Strategy.

Activity 3 – Compare the stories: written with oral re-telling

Aims – Choose words with precision, organise what they say, focus on the main points, sustain concentration, make relevant comments, take turns in speaking.

What to do – Read a story to the children. This can be any text, but try to make sure that it is not too long. Have a short discussion about what happened, the order of events, etc. Now model re-telling the story orally. The children will be quick to pick up differences in your re-telling! Send the children off in small groups or pairs to have a go at re-telling the story themselves.

After they have had time to practise, bring them together. Ask for volunteers, or choose a pair or group who you think re-told the story quite well. Ask them to re-tell their story again but this time into a tape recorder.

Re-read the story and remind the children about the beginning of the lesson and the things everyone discussed. Now play back the recorded oral re-telling. Ask them to compare similarities and differences. You can stop the recorder as they bring up points and then start it again and you can also re-read the part in the story that relates to the part of the re-telling.

This can be done as a whole-class or group activity. If you are fortunate enough to have a lot of tape recorders you can let each small group record their re-telling or, if not, it could perhaps be done over a period of time.

Resources required – At least one tape recorder and audiotape, a short written text for re-telling.

Cross-curricular links – Literacy.

When to do it – During a literacy lesson, either whole class or as group work (guided or independent).

Use of teaching assistants – To support selected groups, general support in the class, offer ideas and prompts during class discussions.

NLS and Foundation Stage

Foundation Stage – Communication, language and literacy

Language for communication
Listen to stories with increasing attention and recall.

Describe main story settings, events and principal characters.

Use language for an increasing range of purposes.

Sustain attentive listening, responding to what they have heard by relevant comments, questions or actions.

Enjoy listening to and using spoken written language, and readily turn to it in their play and learning.

Use a widening range of words to express or elaborate ideas.

Speak clearly and audibly with confidence and control and show awareness of the listener (for example, by their use of conventions such as greetings, 'please' and 'thank you').

Interact with others, negotiating plans and activities and taking turns in conversation.

Language for thinking
Talk activities through, reflecting on and modifying what they are doing.

Use talk to organise, sequence and clarify thinking, ideas, feelings and events.

Reading
Re-tell narratives in the correct sequence, drawing on language patterns of stories.

Reception Year

Text level
T4 To notice the difference between spoken and written forms through re-telling known stories; to compare told versions with what the book 'says'.

T7 To use knowledge of familiar texts to re-enact or re-tell to others, recounting the main points in correct sequence.

Year 1 Term 1 and Term 3

Text level
T3 To notice the difference between spoken and written forms through re-telling known stories; compare oral versions with the written text.

Year 2 Term 1

Text level
T3 To be aware of the difference between spoken and written language through comparing oral recounts with text, make use of formal story elements in re-telling.

Year 2 Term 3

Text level
T3 To notice the difference between spoken and written forms through re-telling known stories; compare oral versions with the written text.

Further comments and suggestions – This is a great way for children to hear the differences between a written text and an oral re-telling. It also offers opportunities for assessment, especially if you have managed to record a number of pairs or groups.

Another way of doing this is for you to re-tell the story orally into the recorder, either when you model it, or have one that you made earlier. You can then use this for the discussion at the end.

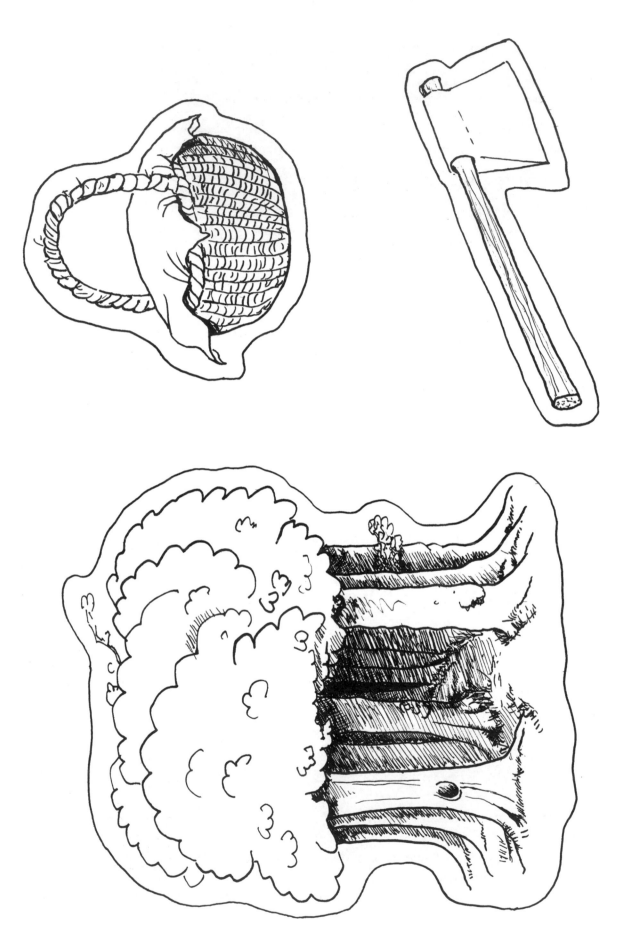

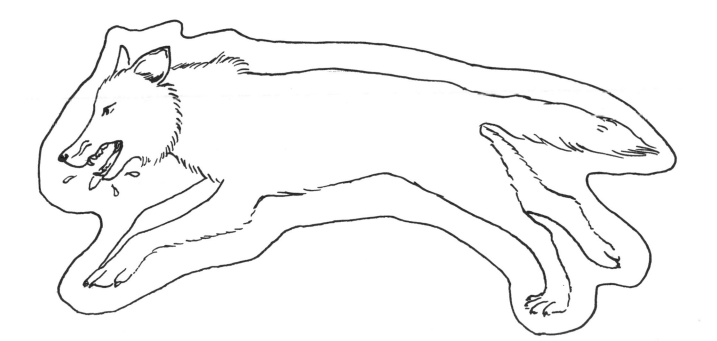

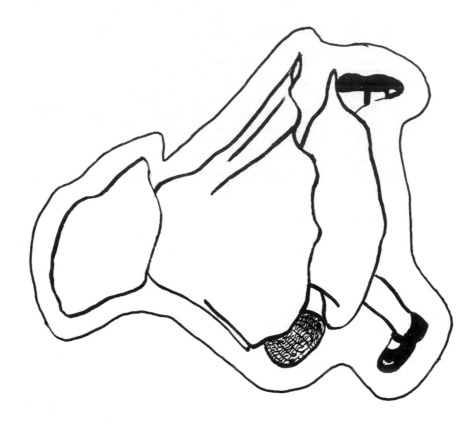

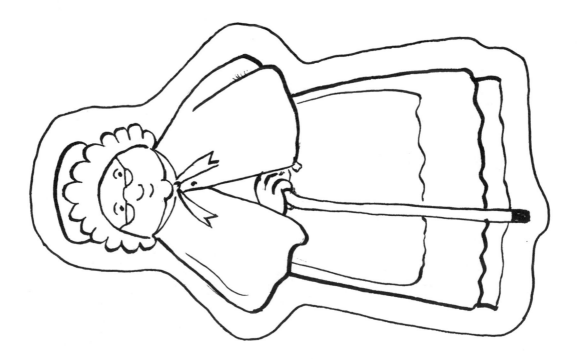

I like using tape recorders with young children because they have not yet reached the stage of not wanting to hear their own voice. I find that it motivates them and helps them to focus on the task.

Story boxes and talk bags and tins

Story boxes, talk bags and talk tins are all quite similar in that they involve children in exploring items (usually about five or six) that have been placed in them. This in itself is excellent for promoting speaking and listening, especially when open questions are included. However, it can be taken a step further by asking the children to actually make up a story inspired by the items.

I have found that young children in particular can find this very challenging. They will often role-play the items literally by moving them around as in small-world play, rather than making the more abstract connection of using the items as a stimulus to base a story on. When I first tried using story boxes I found that the children in my Year 1 class role-played the characters in their boxes, even although some of the items were inanimate, such as a star and a jar of crystals. They used the items very literally. I was not expecting this because my only experience of using story boxes at that time was from working with adults.

In spite of this I thought it was worth having another go because the children had really enjoyed the activity. They loved exploring the boxes and a lot of discussion and talk was generated. I have included the activity here because although the children found it difficult the outcome was extremely successful and the children exceeded all expectations. With support and encouragement they came up with some cracking ideas and although they did not think of complete stories from their boxes we pooled all the ideas and this led to a whole-class story. There was a lot of talk for writing and eventually a fantasy story was produced that every child had contributed towards. The sense of achievement was tremendous.

Activity 4 – A story-box story

Aims – Speak with clear diction and appropriate intonation, choose words with precision, organise what is said, focus on the main points, take into account the needs of their listeners, sustain concentration, take turns in speaking.

What to do – This activity will need to be modelled so the children have a clear understanding of what you are expecting them to do. Place a selection of five to six items that relate to each other in some way in a box for you to share with the children. The items need to have some sort of relationship or theme in order for the activity to work well. The children will be really excited and focused and keen to know what is in the box. Insist that they all sit nicely, and one by one reveal the items.

What you choose to put in the box is up to you. It is a good idea to have worked out your story earlier as it can be quite tricky thinking one up on the spot. This is a good opportunity to work with your TA and show the children how they might collaborate and talk to come up with ideas. Make sure you have met with the TA previously so that they know what to expect.

Tell the children that you are going to use the items to help you make up a story. An example might be as follows: In the box, bag, basket or tin could be a towel (this can be a small hand towel), some sand, a seashell, a ball and a picture of a seahorse, or a plastic toy, a bird's feather, or a plastic toy seagull. Ask the children to suggest what they think the story will be about and they will probably say the sea or the seaside.

An example of what your story could be about follows. It is only a very simple example to give an idea how the items can be used to think up a story.

> Two children go to the beach on holiday (towel and sand). While on the beach the children play with the ball, which was special present from someone (ball). Unfortunately the ball is thrown out to sea and goes bobbing off out of reach in the waves. The children are heartbroken because it was a special ball. The seagulls soaring over the sea hear the children wish for their ball back (feather or toy gull). The seagulls tell the children that the seahorses (picture of seahorse or toy) might be able to help but will require a present in return. The children find a beautiful shell, which the seagulls take to the seahorses and sure enough the children's ball is returned (shell).

Explain to the children that they are going to have a go with their own boxes to try to make up a story, like you did, based on the items in their boxes.

You will need to move from group to group in order to support them and encourage them to think of their story.

At the end of the session bring everyone back to discuss how it went.

Resources required – A selection of boxes, tins or other containers (how many will depend on how you organise your class; I had five, one for each group), items to go in them. If you really want to include something but can't find an example then use a picture.

Cross-curricular links – Literacy.

When to do it – As a group activity in the literacy hour.

Use of teaching assistants – to support selected groups, offer ideas and prompts during class discussions.

NLS and Foundation Stage objectives

Foundation Stage – Communication, language and literacy

Language for communication
Begin to use more complex sentences.

Use language for an increasing range of purposes.

Consistently develop a simple story, explanation or line of questioning.

Listen with enjoyment, and respond to stories, songs and other music, rhymes and poems and make up their own stories, songs, rhymes and poems.

Use a widening range of words to express or elaborate ideas.

Speak clearly and audibly with confidence and control and show awareness of the listener (for example, by their use of conventions such as greetings, 'please' and 'thank you').

Interact with others, negotiating plans and activities and taking turns in conversation.

Language for thinking
Talk activities through, reflecting on and modifying what they are doing.

Use talk to connect ideas, explain what is happening and anticipate what might happen next.

Use talk to pretend imaginary situations.

Use language to imagine and recreate roles and experiences.

Use talk to organise, sequence and clarify thinking, ideas, feelings and events.

Year 1 Term 1

Text level
T7 To re-enact stories in a variety of ways, e.g. through role-play, using dolls or puppets.

Year 1 Term 2

Text level
T7 To discuss reasons for, or causes of, incidents in stories.

Year 1 Term 3

Text level
T5 To re-tell stories, to give the main points in sequence and to pick out significant incidents.

T6 To prepare and re-tell stories orally, identifying and using some of the more formal features of story language.

Year 2 Term 2

Text level
T7 To prepare and re-tell stories individually and through role-play in groups, using dialogue and narrative from text.

PNS objectives – Speaking, listening and learning
Year 1 Term 1

4. Drama
To explore familiar themes and characters through improvisation and role-play, e.g. using story boxes and bags of props to create characters.

Link with NLS text objective 7.

Year 1 Term 2

5. Speaking
To re-tell stories, ordering events using story language, e.g. using different techniques to recall and invent well-structured stories.

Link with NLS text objectives 4 and 5.

7. Group discussion and interaction
To take turns to speak, listen to others' suggestions and talk about what they are going to do, e.g. devising simple rules for turn-taking and contributing in groups.

Year 2 Term 1

15. Group discussion and interaction
To listen to each other's views and preferences, agree the next steps to take and identify contributions by each group member, e.g. learning how to pool views, make decisions and allocate tasks.

Year 2 Term 2

17. Speaking
To tell real and imagined stories using the conventions of familiar story language, e.g. including relevant detail, keeping the listeners' interest and sustaining an account.

Link with NLS text objective 7.

Year 3 Term 2

31. Group discussion and interaction
To actively include and respond to all members of the group, e.g. encouraging contributions by use of questions, eye contact and people's names when discussing an issue.

Year 3 Term 3

36. Drama
To use some drama strategies to explore stories or issues, e.g. working with different techniques to explore key aspects of relationships or situations.

Further comments and suggestions – Remember that young children tend to use the items in the boxes literally by role-playing them. They may find it hard to extend their thought process beyond the physical objects to make up an imaginary story based around them. You will need to make sure that they understand they can make up more things, such as other characters, from their imaginations and do not have to stick only with what they find in the box. I found that children with a wide experience of books and stories, and who were articulate and good at expressing themselves, were able to use the items in a more abstract way.

With younger children, I don't think it matters how they use the boxes; it is the development of language and the ability to order, organise and express their thoughts that is important.

It should be mentioned that not all the items have to be used: one or two can be discarded and the actual container can be part of the story if the children so wish. When working with older children you may decide to have boxes containing different items relating to genres such as ghosts, science fiction, fantasy, etc., and expect them to arrive at a story within those genres. This takes the learning process a step further.

When you are deciding what to place in the boxes, think about the story you would make up around the items. If you find it difficult, it is probable that the children are going to find it even more so. The items need to be something the children can relate to and have some experience of, either in their own lives or from their reading or viewing.

On a health and safety note, make sure the items you put in the boxes are not toxic or likely to cause an allergic reaction. Be aware of the hazards of using small items with young children.

Debating and questioning

This chapter includes:

- Games and activities that require the use of both open and closed questions

- Ideas for questions across the curriculum

- Two different ways of organising debates.

Questioning

The role of questioning is a vital one in helping children to learn. Not only does it help children to think carefully and become independent learners but it is also important in providing teachers with opportunities to assess children's understanding and their way of thinking. Questions are usually referred to as being either 'open' or 'closed'. An open question is one that requires children to reflect and think about the answer, whereas a closed question often can be answered in one or two words such as 'Green' in answer to 'What colour is the grass?' Asking as many open questions as possible is important as it helps develop and extend children's thinking skills.

I have always tried to provide opportunities for a variety of talk in my classroom as well as providing an interesting stimulus to start with. Some of the activities I have included in this section may seem obvious and probably go on in lots of classrooms but some may not be quite so usual to use with young children. The activities include both open and closed questioning that involves the children themselves in questioning and answering, as well as the teacher. Some of the activities encompass an element of both debate and questioning.

Activity 1 – Share your news/show and tell

Aims – speak clearly, organise what they say, take into account the needs of their listeners, sustain concentration, remember specific points that interest them, make relevant comments, take turns in speaking.

66

What to do – Sit the children in a circle (older children may prefer to sit at their tables). Explain that this is an opportunity for them to share some news if they want. Tell them that they must sit and listen carefully to their friends and must not shout out or interrupt. They can put their hands up when the speaker has finished to make relevant comments or ask any questions.

Choose a child to begin and let them stand up and share their news or show an object. Some children are very clear and focused about what they want to say but others find it harder to express themselves. This sort of activity helps children practise organising their thoughts in a non-threatening situation. I usually tell the children I want them to have thought carefully of what they are going to say before they say it, and insist upon clear sentences. This helps them to focus on organising their speech and using appropriate language. If a child is struggling you can quietly prompt them.

After the child has finished speaking, ask the class if anyone would like to make any comments about what has been said or ask any relevant questions. The children need to really listen to what is being said in order to do this. Make sure any questions and comments are actually relevant and not a way in to sharing their own news before they are chosen.

Children will often ask a question that has already been answered in the initial sentence, for instance, 'My mum got me this teddy from the market', and a child asks, 'Where did you get it from?' Remind the children, when this happens, that this is why they need to listen really carefully.

This activity can take time but try to ensure that all the children get a turn over the course of the year.

Resources required – None.

Cross-curricular links – English and any subject that the news might be connected with, such as RE, PSHE.

When to do it – In a regular slot either after a lesson when there are ten minutes to spare, before break, during milk and snack time or straight after lunch.

Use of teaching assistants – Ensure the rest of the class are listening carefully, suggest which child might like to have the next turn.

NLS and Foundation Stage objectives

Foundation Stage – Communication, language and literacy

Language for communication
Use intonation, rhythm and phrasing to make their meaning clear to others.

Begin to use more complex sentences.

Use language for an increasing range of purposes.

Sustain attentive listening, responding to what they have heard by relevant comments, questions or actions.

Ask simple questions, often in the form of 'what' or 'where'?

Speak clearly and audibly with confidence and control and show awareness of the listener, for example by their use of conventions such as greetings, 'please' and 'thank you'.

PNS objectives – Speaking, listening and learning

Year 1 Term 1

1. Speaking

To describe incidents or tell stories from their own experience, in an audible voice, e.g. recounting events using detail, following teacher modelling.

Link with NLS text objectives 5 and 9.

2. Listening

To listen with sustained concentration, e.g. identifying points of interest when listening to an explanation.

Year 2 Term 1

14. Listening

To listen to others in class, ask relevant questions and follow instructions, e.g. listening to and questioning instructions for devising a game.

Further comments and suggestions – This is a really simple activity but be aware that sometimes a child may say something that is a cause for concern or may need handling sensitively. If this happens make a mental note to yourself to follow it up or get someone else such as a TA to do it for you. Finding time to do this activity may be difficult but I think it is well worth fitting it in if possible because for those few minutes that one child can feel really important and special and it is a great boost to self-esteem.

There can be good opportunities within this activity for you to model open questions. News such as, 'I went to Great Yarmouth at the weekend' will often promote questions from children such as, 'Was it nice?' This can really only be answered with a yes or no. The teacher can extend the child's answer by asking questions such as, 'What did you do there?', 'What did you like best and why?', 'Why did you go?', 'What did you see?'. This helps model different sorts of questioning for the rest of the class.

Not all children want to participate but if the activity is a regular event then even the quietest of children will eventually offer to share something. Children generally love to talk about themselves and their families, and this is a good way to engage them.

The next activity has been adapted from a well-known party game which, although it involves use of closed questions, requires the children to think hard about what they have heard and apply it to their questioning in order to work out the answer. It is also good fun and the children really enjoy it.

Activity 2 – Twenty questions (or thereabout!)

Aims – Choose words with precision, focus on the main points, use appropriate questioning, take turns in speaking, develop use of subject-specific vocabulary.

What to do – tell the children they are going to play a guessing game that involves asking questions to work out a 'mystery' object. It is a good idea to decide on a subject area or topic within which the object fits. This narrows down the choices and helps focus the children's thoughts.

Discuss with the children what the topic will be and when they have decided explain that you are going to think of something to do with the topic and they have to work out what it is. If the topic is 'light and dark' in science, you might think of a torch.

Next ask the children to think of questions that might help them decide what it is. You will probably find that the children will begin to guess wildly at first, without using questions to reduce the possibilities. Remind them of the sorts of questions they could ask to narrow it down, such as 'is this thing a natural light source?' Or 'does it work with batteries?'

After each question do a tally on the board so the children can see how many questions they have used up. When the item has been guessed, someone else has a turn.

You can make up your own rules and adapt the game as you want. You can say that the person giving the answers can only answer yes or no, which makes it more difficult for the questioners. This might be too difficult for some children and so you could allow more information to be given in the answer, but they must be careful not to give too much away.

Resources required – None.

Cross-curricular links – All subjects.

When to do it – At the end of the day, before the class goes home, before lunch, at any time when there are the odd five minutes to fill, briefly at the end of a lesson, or near the end of a topic to reinforce artefacts used.

Use of teaching assistants – To prompt and support children with questions and ideas, to sit with and support a small targeted group or individuals.

NLS and Foundation Stage objectives
Foundation Stage – Communication, language and literacy
Language for communication
Use language for an increasing range of purposes.

Sustain attentive listening, responding to what they have heard by relevant comments, questions or actions.

Ask simple questions, often in the form of 'what' or 'where'?

Respond to simple instructions.

Speak clearly and audibly with confidence and control and show awareness of the listener, for example by their use of conventions such as greetings, 'please' and 'thank you'.

Interact with others, negotiating plans and activities and taking turns in conversation.

Further comments and suggestions – Children really engage well with this game, especially older ones. I have played it a lot with Year 3 and have found that boys in particular enjoy it. Things can become quite heated when the questions are running out and someone wastes one by asking something that has already been asked! It is also great for reminding the children about what they have been learning as you can have a brief discussion about the mystery item when it has been guessed.

There are no resources needed to play this game; however, you may want the child to tell you what their item is so that you can help, if necessary, with the answers. It also helps to eliminate any cheating.

Activity 3 – What's my number?

Aims – choose words with precision, focus on the main points, use appropriate questioning, take turns in speaking, develop use of subject-specific vocabulary.

What to do – Tell the children you are a number and they are to guess which one. It will depend on the age and ability of the children as to the number you choose. It might be any number or a number within a set range, for instance between 1 and 20.

Explain that you want them to find out the number by asking questions and working it out from the answers and not just by guessing. Model some of the questions they could use, e.g. 'Are you an odd or even number?' 'How many digits do you have?' 'Are you a number in the teens?'

When the children have found your number, choose one of them to be the number and repeat the process.

Resources required – None.

Cross-curricular links – English, maths.

When to do it – As part of the oral warm-up in a maths lesson, whenever there are a few minutes to spare during the school day, before lunch, before home time, etc.

Use of teaching assistants – To prompt and support children with questions and ideas, to sit with and support a small, targeted group or individual.

NLS and Foundation Stage objectives

Foundation Stage — Communication, language and literacy

Language for communication
Use language for an increasing range of purposes.

Sustain attentive listening, responding to what they have heard by relevant comments, questions or actions.

Ask simple questions, often in the form of 'what' or 'where'?

Respond to simple instructions.

Language for thinking
Talk activities through, reflecting on and modifying what they are doing.

Use talk to connect ideas, explain what is happening and anticipate what might happen next.

PNS objectives — Speaking, listening and learning

Year 1 Term 1

3. Group discussion and interaction
To ask and answer questions, make relevant contributions, offer suggestions and take turns, e.g. when devising ways of sorting items in the classroom.

Year 2 Term 1

14. Listening
To listen to others in class, ask relevant questions and follow instructions, e.g. listening to and questioning instructions for devising a game.

Further comments and suggestions – I find that children enjoy this activity and their questioning improves the more they do it. It also helps develop their knowledge of numbers and number recognition.

Questions across the curriculum

It is probably true to say that most teachers ask if there are any questions, after they have taught a lesson or explained an activity, and children tend to respond with questions to help them do the activity such as 'do we have to sit in our groups?' Questions that enquire about or question what has just been taught are more rare. In my own classroom children would seldom question anything I said or even ask what something meant. Most of us have experienced the situation when they have stopped in the middle of reading a story or an explanation, to ask what a word or phrase means, to be met with blank stares and stony silence.

Children need to feel comfortable with the idea of asking questions, in an environment where they feel they will not be made fun of. They also need to experience the sorts of questions that we, as teachers, would like them to ask. The best way of doing this is by modelling it. As already mentioned, we need to ask children as many open questions as possible which require them to think about the answers and query them. Practical and investigative activities such as those described in Chapter 2 of this book provide some excellent opportunities for these sorts of questions. An example of open questions in those sorts of lessons might be:

> What colours could you use to match that piece of material?
> How can you fix this piece of card to that piece of plastic? Can you think of another way?
> What do you think this object was used for? How can you find out?
> Why do you think this piece of paper can be pleated but this piece of card cannot?
> What can you see through the magnifying glass that you can't without it?
> Are there any other materials we can investigate? Where might we find them?
> Can you tell me what you can see? Why do you think that is?
> Wow! That's brilliant; tell me how you managed to do it!

Once children hear these sorts of questions being asked by the teacher they begin to start using them themselves, both to adults and each other.

The subject of questioning is also raised in Chapters 3 and 6 of this book in relation to hot-seating and picture books.

Debating

Holding a debate is perhaps not an activity that readily springs to mind when thinking of activities to do with 5- and 6-year-olds but it is one of the activities suggested in the PNS Speaking, listening and learning materials.

I had not considered using debate with young children until a few years ago when it was suggested I try it out with my Year 1 class. I have to admit that at the time I was pretty sceptical as to what the outcome would be but soon came to realise that this is a powerful tool in developing children's language as well as engaging them in meaningful discussion.

I introduced the children to the idea of discussion and thinking about issues through a form of 'conscience alley'. A conscience alley is where two lines of children are formed and another child walks between the lines in role. The children voice the thoughts of the character to try to persuade them to make a decision or take a particular course of action. I adapted this and changed it into a debate.

Activity 4 – Should Goldilocks have gone into the bears' house?

Aims – choose words with precision and organise what is said, sustain concentration, listen to others' reactions, make relevant comments, take turns in speaking, relate their contributions to what has gone before, take different views into account, extend their ideas in the light of discussion, give reasons for opinions.

What to do – Divide the class into two groups. Try to have a balance of both confident, articulate children and those that are less so in each group. Sit them at either side of the room with a space between them. This helps to differentiate the two views being debated. Explain that one group has to give reasons why Goldilocks should not have gone into the bears' house, and the other group why she was right to have done so.

When this has been decided let the debate begin. Ask for someone to start the debate from either side. As with other activities, make sure the children listen to each other and do not interrupt.

When you feel that the subject has been discussed fully you can make a decision as to which argument was the most persuasive.

Resources required – None.

Cross-curricular links – Literacy.

When to do it – As part of a unit of work in literacy on traditional stories.

Use of teaching assistants – To support one of the groups in the debate, to offer a second opinion on which side offered the most persuasive debate, support the teacher by monitoring behaviour.

NLS and Foundation Stage objectives

Foundation Stage – Communication, language and literacy

Language for communication
Begin to use more complex sentences.

Use language for an increasing range of purposes.

Sustain attentive listening, responding to what they have heard by relevant comments, questions or actions.

Question why things happen, and give explanations.

Initiate conversation, attend to and take account of what others say, and use talk to resolve disagreement.

Use a widening range of words to express or elaborate ideas.

Speak clearly and audibly with confidence and control and show awareness of the listener (for example by their use of conventions such as greetings, 'please' and 'thank you').

Interact with others, negotiating plans and activities and taking turns in conversation.

Language for thinking
Use talk to connect ideas, explain what is happening and anticipate what might happen next.

Begin to use talk, instead of action to rehearse, reorder and reflect on past experience, linking significant events from own experience and from stories, paying attention to sequence and how events lead into one another.

Use talk to organise, sequence and clarify thinking, ideas, feelings and events.

Year 3 Term 3

Text level
T5 To discuss (i) characters' feelings; (ii) behaviour, e.g. fair or unreasonable, brave or foolish; (iii) relationships, referring to the text and making judgements.

PNS objectives – Speaking, listening and learning

Year 1 Term 1

2. Listening
To listen with sustained concentration, e.g. identifying points of interest when listening to an explanation.

3. Group discussion and interaction
To ask and answer questions, make relevant contributions, offer suggestions and take turns, e.g. when devising ways of sorting items in the classroom.

Year 3 Term 1

26. Listening
To follow up others' points and show whether they agree or disagree in a whole-class discussion, e.g. working together as a whole class to generate ideas for writing.

Year 3 Term 2

31. Group discussion and interaction
To actively include and respond to all members of the group, e.g. encouraging contributions by use of questions, eye contact and people's names when discussing an issue.

Year 3 Term 3

33. Speaking
To sustain conversation, explaining or giving reasons for their views or choices, e.g. making extended contributions when explaining solutions to problems or choosing equipment for a classroom task.

> *35. Group discussion and interaction*
> To use the language of possibility to investigate and reflect on feelings, behaviour or relationships, e.g. investigating and reflecting on the interactions between characters when reading a story.
>
> Link with NLS text objective 5.

Further comments and suggestions – When I carried out this activity the children found it easier to argue that Goldilocks should not have gone into the house, but there were also some good reasons given as to why she was right to have gone in. Everyone really enjoyed it.

You may find that you need to remind the children which side of the debate they are on as I found when one child made an excellent point but it was a view that helped the opposite side!

The more the children do this, the better they get. They really get into the idea of debating and arguments can become quite heated. It also improves their ability to justify their statements.

Other successful debates for me have been, 'Who are best, boys or girls?' and 'Is the Big Bad Wolf really bad?' There are many subjects that you could set up as a debate. It may depend to some extent on the age of the children as to what you might choose to do.

I carried out a debate on a more serious topic and was amazed at the response I got from the children. I have included it here because of how successful it was but you will need to adapt it to your own school's circumstances. You may have to change the subject of the debate but try to base it on something that could affect the children and their community if it were to happen. You might be in a situation where there is already something controversial being proposed, in which case you could use that.

I set up the debate by asking the children to pretend that there was a proposal to build a new take-away outlet at the local shops. Existing already on this site are a number of shops, an off-licence, a family centre, a playgroup and an underpass that leads through to the middle school and adjacent housing estate, all of which the children are very familiar with. On this occasion I did not split the class into groups but allowed the children to voice their opinions as a whole. The only stipulation was that I wanted to hear views that expressed both sides of the argument.

This activity is good to use at Key Stage 2, as is the next.

Activity 5 – Should a take-away be built at the local shops?

Aims – Choose words with precision and organise what is said, sustain concentration, listen to others' reactions, make relevant comments, take turns in speaking, relate their contributions to what has gone before, take different views into account, extend their ideas in the light of discussion, give reasons for opinions.

What to do – Seat the children in front of you or at their tables if you prefer. Explain that you want them to pretend that a take-away is to be built at their local shops. Ask them to think carefully about the implications of this. Would it be a good or a bad thing to happen? You might have to give them an example of the sort of issues they need to think about to start them off, such as how useful it would be to have a take-away outlet.

Give the children some time to think about it and then start taking their comments. You can write them on either the whiteboard or a large piece of paper if you want to keep them. Those of you with interactive whiteboards in the classroom can save the comments on that. Divide the paper or board into two columns, one for and one against; then you get a clear picture of how the debate is going.

Keep the debate lively. Encourage the children when they offer comments by positive responses and use open questions to really get them to think about and justify their statements. If a child suggests a reason why it is not a good idea, get some suggestions for why it might be a good idea. You might say, 'Right, Nazia thinks it is not a good idea, and has given us a really good reason why but what does anyone else think? Does anyone here like take-away food? Do your grown-ups ever have take-aways? Someone give me a reason why there should be a take-away built at the shops.'

By countering each comment and challenging the children you are modelling how to really get into the debate and the children will respond appropriately.

Resources required – Something to record the children's comments on.

Cross-curricular links – All subjects, particularly history, geography, English.

When to do it – Integrated into a lesson where the topic is appropriate. This debate formed part of a Year 1 geography lesson on the local area.

Use of teaching assistants – To encourage children with their comments, working with individuals or selected groups, noting down the comments while the teacher manages the debate.

NLS and Foundation Stage objectives

Foundation Stage – Communication, language and literacy

Language for communication
Use language for an increasing range of purposes.

Sustain attentive listening, responding to what they have heard by relevant comments, questions or actions.

Initiate conversation, attend to and take account of what others say, and use talk to resolve disagreement.

Use a widening range of words to express or elaborate ideas.

Speak clearly and audibly with confidence and control and show awareness of the listener (for example, by use of conventions such as greetings, 'please' and 'thank you').

Interact with others, negotiating plans and activities and taking turns in conversation.

Language for thinking
Use talk to pretend imaginary situations.

Use talk to organise, sequence and clarify thinking, ideas, feelings and events.

PNS objectives – Speaking, listening and learning
Year 1 Term 1

2. Listening
To listen with sustained concentration, e.g. identifying points of interest when listening to an explanation.

3. Group discussion and interaction
To ask and answer questions, make relevant contributions, offer suggestions and take turns, e.g. when devising ways of sorting items in the classroom.

Year 3 Term 1

26. Listening
To follow up others' points and show whether they agree or disagree in a whole-class discussion, e.g. working together as a whole class to generate ideas for writing.

Year 3 Term 2

31. Group discussion and interaction
To actively include and respond to all members of the group, e.g. encouraging contributions by use of questions, eye contact and people's names when discussing an issue.

Year 3 Term 3

33. Speaking
To sustain conversation, explaining or giving reasons for their views or choices, e.g. making extended contributions when explaining solutions to problems or choosing equipment for a classroom task.

Further comments and suggestions – The language and discussion that this debate generated was phenomenal. The children I work with often seem unable to use their language abilities in 'school mode'; by grounding the debate in experiences the children have of everyday life they were able to use their language and reasoning abilities to good effect.

I have sometimes heard teachers suggest that they cannot carry out activities involving talk and discussions because the children do not have the language for it. I think as teachers it is important to develop a 'can do' culture with our children. Possibly it is not that children don't have the language but more that they have to learn how to use language in a school setting.

Pictures and picture books

This chapter includes:

- How to use a painting to encourage prediction and discussion

- Drama activities from a painting

- Drawing a picture as it is described

- Using picture books and discussing illustrations

- Using visual image as a narrative.

In this chapter I will be describing activities that are based on the visual image. Most of them are very simple, involving the use of pictures and picture books and can be carried out easily in all classrooms. It is an effective way to engage children and helps to develop their language skills through discussion. The idea is based on the premise that a visual image, whether moving or still, tells a story and therefore becomes a visual text. I have included NLS objectives that relate to written text but which can easily be adapted and applied to visual images.

Pictures and paintings

A few years ago I had the good fortune to attend a CPD course for teachers at the National Gallery in London. The course, 'Take One Picture', focuses on one particular painting and cross-curricular ways to use it are modelled. I would strongly recommend anyone to go on the course should they be given the opportunity, as it is inspiring.

The first activity is from an idea suggested on the course. In this activity I used a print of the painting 'St George and the Dragon' by Paolo Uccello; however, the same principle can be applied to any picture.

Activity 1 – Guess the picture

Aims – To encourage participation, speak clearly, choose words with precision and organise what is said, make relevant comments, listen to others' reactions, take turns in speaking, relate their contributions to what has gone before, take different views into account, give reasons for opinions.

What to do – Find a picture that you think will engage the children either because of what it shows or because of the story behind it. This could be a fine-art print from the school resources, or one of your own. A photograph or still from a film would be suitable but it needs to be big enough for the children to see quite clearly.

Place a piece of card or thick paper over the image with some 'doors' cut out of it. The doors need to be big enough to allow some of the picture behind to show but not so big as to give too much away. I made the doors so that they could be opened like an Advent calendar. You can decide how many doors to have. I cut three out on this occasion. Be selective about which parts of the picture will show through the doors. There needs to be something seen that will arouse the children's curiosity and catch their attention.

Make a mystery about what is hidden behind the card. Tell the children that they are going to be picture detectives and will try to predict what the whole picture is, but they will only be given a few clues like a real detective. You will find that they will really get into the spirit of the activity and will be keen to know what the hidden image is.

Open a door and ask the children to describe what they can see. At this point they may try to predict what the image is but they will not have a lot to go on. After a while when you feel the children have got as much as they are going to from that particular door, open another, and then the last. The children will be desperate for you to reveal the whole picture.

I make them wait until the next day before they find out what the picture is. There is always a groan when I do this but they are really focused and ready for their lesson the next day!

Resources required – A picture, large enough for the children to make out details quite easily. A piece of card with doors cut out of it in appropriate places, a means of fastening it all in place such as clips or Blu-tac℗.

Cross-curricular links – Any subject that can be related to the picture being used; an example might be history if using a painting set in the past.

When to do it – As part of the introduction to a topic or as a visual stimulus within a topic, as a visual text in the literacy hour.

Use of teaching assistants – To prompt and support individuals or selected groups.

NLS and Foundation Stage objectives
Foundation Stage – Communication, language and literacy
Language for communication
Begin to use more complex sentences.

Use language for an increasing range of purposes.

Sustain attentive listening, responding to what they have heard by relevant comments, questions or actions.

Ask simple questions, often in the form of 'what' or 'where'?

Use a widening range of words to express or elaborate ideas.

Speak clearly and audibly with confidence and control and show awareness of the listener (for example, by use of conventions such as greetings, 'please' and 'thank you').

Interact with others, negotiating plans and activities and taking turns in conversation.

Language for thinking
Use talk to connect ideas, explain what is happening and anticipate what might happen next.

Suggest how the story might end.

Year 1 Term 2

Text level
T7 To discuss reasons for, or causes of, incidents in stories.

T8 To identify and discuss characters, e.g. appearance, behaviour, qualities; to speculate about how they might behave; to discuss how they are described in the text; and to compare characters from different stories or plays.

Year 2 Term 2

Text level
T3 To discuss and compare story themes.

T4 To predict story endings/incidents, e.g. from unfinished extracts, while reading with the teacher.

T5 To discuss story settings; to compare differences; to locate key words and phrases in text; to consider how different settings influence events and behaviour.

T6 To identify and describe characters, expressing own views and using words and phrases from texts.

Year 3 Term 3

Text level
T5 To discuss (i) characters' feelings; (ii) behaviour, e.g. fair or unreasonable, brave or foolish; (iii) relationships, referring to the text and making judgements.

Further comments and suggestions – The first time I did this activity I was amazed at how much the children engaged with it. They drew on their own previous knowledge and understanding to make their predictions. Their guesses were based on sensible reasoning and they were able to justify their suggestions. They referred to books and films and computer games they knew. I have since repeated the activity with different classes and different pictures and have always had a brilliant response. Colleagues who have done the same in their classes have met with a similar response and one colleague working with a Year 3 class found that not only did it help develop talk and discussion but it was an excellent stimulus for writing.

After the picture was revealed the discussion did not stop; indeed, it became more animated as the children learnt more about the painting and the artist.

I used freeze-frames in an extension of the activity as a means of getting the children to really think about the characters and what was happening in the picture. It also helped them decide what might happen next. If you decide that you want the children to use prediction as part of the work you are doing, you will need to ensure that the picture you are using does not have a story that the children know. I did not tell the children the story of St George and the Dragon until we had explored the picture in lots of ways and they had formulated their own ideas about what was happening. How this activity works and the outcomes from it will very much depend on the picture you use.

Freeze-frames

A 'freeze-frame' is a silent tableau that shows a specific event or incident. It involves children either individually or in groups representing the characters at a set moment in time. If you think of a film being stopped with all the characters in the frame at that time motionless then you can get an idea of what is meant by freeze-frame. The event could be a real one such as an incident from history, or from a fictional story. In these situations you would have to position the 'characters' yourself. If you use a painting then the characters are already positioned for you.

I used the Uccello painting for freeze-framing but as already mentioned, many pictures can be used as effectively following the same ideas.

Activity 2 – Freeze-frame from a painting

Aims – Choose words with precision, organise what is said, focus on the main points, sustain concentration, make relevant comments, listen to others' reactions, take turns in speaking, relate their contributions to what has gone before, create and sustain roles individually and when working with others.

What to do – It is really important for this activity to be demonstrated and for the children to know the purpose of it. They need to know why they are doing it and what they will be learning from it as well as it being an enjoyable activity which is fun to do.

This activity ideally should be carried out after the previous one because by now the children will have become familiar with whatever painting or picture you are using. They will already have discussed what they think is happening and who they think the characters

---

are. Explain that they are now going to really think hard about the characters and what they might be thinking and feeling, and to help, they are going to make a freeze-frame.

Explain this by modelling it. Seat the class in a large horseshoe, ensuring that they can all see. Select some children who you feel will be able to manage the activity sensibly and who will be able to model it well. Show them how to make a tableau using the painting as a guide. This is a good opportunity to reinforce prepositions: ask the class where the children need to stand to make the picture, for example, next to, behind, in front of, etc.

Be aware that some children can find this quite challenging. I found that a number of children could not put themselves into the same positions as the characters in the painting without support.

Explain to the class when they have made their tableau they need to think hard about their character. Tell them they will need to consider how their character might be feeling and what they might be thinking.

After the children have made their tableau and you have given them time to think, ask them to sit down in their groups and talk to each other about their thoughts. Walk around the groups and listen to what they are saying and make a note of any particularly good comments. At the end bring the class together and ask for any contributions. You can prompt and encourage the children using the comments you heard and from your observations.

I made this a whole-class activity as part of my literacy hour. If you are not very confident with the idea of freeze-frames you may decide to try it out first with one small group.

Resources required – A painting, picture, or other visual image such as a film still.

Cross-curricular links – Any subject that can be linked to the visual image being used.

When to do it – As part of the introduction to a topic or as a visual stimulus within a topic, in literacy to explore characters from books and visual texts.

Use of teaching assistants – To prompt and support individuals or selected groups, to be another listener and observer when the children are discussing their work in groups.

NLS and Foundation Stage objectives

Foundation Stage – Communication, language and literacy

Language for communication
Use language for an increasing range of purposes.

Sustain attentive listening, responding to what they have heard by relevant comments, questions or actions.

Question why things happen, and give explanations.

Use a widening range of words to express or elaborate ideas.

Interact with others, negotiating plans and activities and taking turns in conversation.

Language for thinking

Talk activities through, reflecting on and modifying what they are doing.

Use talk to connect ideas, explain what is happening and anticipate what might happen next.

Year 1 Term 2

Text level

T8 To identify and discuss characters, e.g. appearance, behaviour, qualities; to speculate about how they might behave; to discuss how they are described in the text; and to compare characters from different stories or plays.

T9 To become aware of character and dialogue, e.g. by role-playing parts when reading aloud stories or plays with others.

Year 1 Term 3

Text level

T5 To re-tell stories, to give the main points in sequence and to pick out significant incidents.

Year 2 Term 2

Text level

T4 To predict story endings/incidents, e.g. from unfinished extracts (while reading with the teacher).

Year 3 Term 3

Text level

T5 To discuss (i) characters' feelings; (ii) behaviour, e.g. fair or unreasonable, brave or foolish; (iii) relationships, referring to the text and making judgements.

Further comments and suggestions – Once the children are familiar with the idea of freeze-frames any subsequent activities should be easier to implement. A natural extension of this activity is to use drama to role-play what happened next.

You will become more confident each time you do the activity. Remember, as with all the activities in the book, if it goes wrong, never mind, evaluate the lesson, concentrate on what was good and have another go. We try to encourage children to take risks and teach them that we can learn from our mistakes, so we should do the same.

Pictures or film stills also make an excellent stimulus for predicting what might happen next or what happened previously. They provide opportunities for children to use language to say what they think and to justify their statements.

The next activity ties in nicely with the previous two. Any picture can be used but it should be one that the children have not seen before. This activity is great for enhancing listening skills as well as requiring the speakers to really think carefully about what they have to say.

Activity 3 – Visualise and draw a described picture

Aims – Speak clearly, choose words with precision, organise what they say, take into account the needs of the listeners, sustain concentration, follow instructions, ask questions to clarify their understanding.

What to do – Seat the children at their tables and provide them with a piece of paper and a pencil. Place a picture where they can't see it but where they can hear someone describe it. One way is to attach it to a small, free-standing whiteboard that can be moved near to the tables with the picture facing away from the class.

Choose a child to describe the picture. This is not as easy as it may seem; I would suggest you choose an articulate child to start with. I have sometimes had two children together as they can help each other and it's not quite so daunting.

The children need to describe the picture so that their classmates can draw it as accurately as possible on their pieces of paper. They should describe a part at a time and allow the class time to draw it. You will probably have to offer some support both to the drawers and the describers but this will depend on the age and ability of the class.

When you feel the children have done enough, stop the session. Ask the class what, if anything, they found particularly difficult. Ask the describers what problems they had, and what would they do differently next time to make describing the picture easier for the class to understand.

Now turn the painting around and let the children see how they got on. This in itself will generate more discussion as they compare their drawings. Older children may take the describers to task if they feel they were given an incorrect or unclear instruction.

Resources required – A picture to describe (this can be any but a fine-art print is ideal), pencils, paper.

Cross-curricular links – Art, literacy, history.

When to do it – As part of an introduction to a particular artist or painting, as an introduction to a visual text/genre in literacy, as an introduction to a particular topic or period in history.

Use of teaching assistants – To support individuals in the class, encourage children to listen carefully and to remain focused.

NLS and Foundation Stage objectives

Foundation Stage – Communication, language and literacy

Language for communication
Begin to use more complex sentences.

Describe main story settings, events and principal characters (as a visual story).

Use language for an increasing range of purposes.

Sustain attentive listening, responding to what they have heard by relevant comments, questions or actions.

Ask simple questions, often in the form of 'what' or 'where'?

Respond to simple instructions.

Use a widening range of words to express or elaborate ideas.

Year 1 Term 1

Text level

T5 To describe story settings and incidents and relate them to own experience and that of others.

PNS objectives – Speaking, listening and learning

Year 1 Term 1

1. Speaking

To describe incidents or tell stories from their own experience, in an audible voice, e.g. recounting events using detail, following teacher modelling.

Link with NLS text objectives 5 and 9.

Year 1 Term 2

6. Listening

To listen and follow instructions accurately, asking for help and clarification if necessary, e.g. learning about the purpose of instructions, devising and following more complex instructions.

Further comments and suggestions – There are a number of variations of this activity. You could ask the children to use colour so that the describers also have to consider that in their description. This however can have resource implications; for example, if all the children reach for a green pencil after being told to draw a green field in the background, are there enough green pencils?

It is not until you do this yourself that you realise how difficult it is. It is excellent for using prepositions and reinforcing left and right, as well as introducing subject-specific vocabulary such as foreground, mid-ground and background.

Picture books

The scope for using picture books for developing children's language is phenomenal. A good picture book works on many levels and should be appreciated and enjoyed by all ages. I use picture books extensively in my teaching and regret that they often are regarded as unsuitable for children much over the age of 7 because they are perceived as 'too easy'. A good picture book can often be as challenging as, or more so, than its non-illustrated counterpart.

There is no 'set' activity that I have carried out with picture books. I use them all the time in a variety of situations.

Activity 4 – Talking about a picture book (whole class)

Aims – Choose words with precision, include relevant detail, answer questions appropriately, ask questions to clarify their understanding, sustain concentration, make relevant comments, give reasons for opinions and actions.

What to do – Select a book that you think the children will enjoy. This will most probably be one of your own favourites, which is a good idea. We all teach better when we love the text being used and want others to share our enthusiasm. It can be one the children have not heard before or an old favourite. If you are not comfortable reading aloud to a class, or have not had much experience of it, decide on a book that you are confident with.

Most children, however restless, will enjoy listening to a story, especially if it is read in an exciting way that keeps their attention. I have taught some very challenging children at times but have not yet experienced a child who cannot be drawn into a story that is read with lots of expression and intonation.

Ensure that they are all sitting where they can see you and the book, and where you can see all of them. Most children at Key Stage 1 and the Foundation Stage are used to sitting on the carpet in front of the teacher. If you teach older children they may be used to sitting at their tables but as the illustrations are paramount to the story in a good picture book, all the children should be close enough to see them.

Begin by looking at the front cover. Cover the title and ask the children to predict what they think the story might be about just from the cover illustration. Next read the title together and ask them if that has changed their first ideas.

After that have a look at the end papers. Some books have end papers that are an integral part of the whole book design and are important to the story. Discuss how they think the end papers contribute to the text.

Hold the book up and to one side so the children can see the illustrations as you read the written text. As you read, put as much variety and expression into your voice as possible and if there is dialogue try to give the characters different voices. This can be difficult as you may get mixed up with which voice belongs to which character. Don't let this put you off; the more you do it the better you get.

Stop at the illustrations and ask the children what they can see, or what they think is happening. Try to ask open questions that require the children to think about the answers and give more than one word answers. Questions you might ask are:

How do you think the character is feeling?
What is in the text that makes you think that?

What could be another title for this book?

How would you have felt?

What would you have done?

What do you think happens in the end? (Before you finish the book!)

What can you see in the illustration?

What do you think the illustration is telling us? Is it telling us anything more than the written text?

Does this book remind you of any others you have read/heard?

Have you seen illustrations like these before?

This is only a sample, and of course the questions you or the children ask will depend on the story and the situation.

Resources required – Picture books (examples given in the References).

Cross-curricular links – All subjects depending on the subject or story line of the book.

When to do it – After playtime, after lunchtime, before home time, at the beginning of a lesson as an introduction or a link to the lesson content.

Use of teaching assistants – Supporting groups or individuals to listen, answer and ask questions.

NLS and Foundation Stage objectives

Foundation Stage – Communication, language and literacy

Language for communication
Begin to use more complex sentences.

Use language for an increasing range of purposes.

Sustain attentive listening, responding to what they have heard by relevant comments, questions or actions.

Ask simple questions, often in the form of 'what' or 'where'?

Use a widening range of words to express or elaborate ideas.

Language for thinking
Use talk to connect ideas, explain what is happening and anticipate what might happen next.

Suggest how the story might end.

Year 1 Term 2

Text level
T6 To identify and discuss a range of story themes, and to collect and compare.

T7 To discuss reasons for, or causes of, incidents in stories.

T8 To identify and discuss characters, e.g. appearance, behaviour, qualities; to speculate about how they might behave; to discuss how they are described in the text; and to compare characters from different stories or plays.

Year 2 Term 2

Text level

T3 To discuss and compare story themes.

T4 To predict story endings/incidents, e.g. from unfinished extracts, while reading with the teacher.

T5 To discuss story settings; to compare differences; to locate key words and phrases in text; to consider how different settings influence events and behaviour.

T6 To identify and describe characters, expressing own views and using words and phrases from texts.

Further comments and suggestions – Try to choose a story that leaves 'gaps' in the text for the reader, or in this case the listeners, to fill, in order to work out and enjoy what the author/illustrator has not said but merely implied. Many picture books do this, and in addition require the illustrations to be 'read' to understand the full meaning of the book.

I have included a list of books that do this well at the end of this book.

Using a picture book with the whole class works in a slightly different way than when you share it with an individual or small group. In that situation the setting is more intimate which makes it easier to include everyone and ensure his or her views are heard.

The illustrations can also be harder to see for those children sitting at the back in a whole-class setting, especially if they are very detailed. It is essential that the pictures can be seen because understanding the story in the best picture books requires the reader to be able to interpret the illustrations and this skill applies even more so to wordless picture books.

Children can find wordless picture books very challenging although they are often assumed to be less important or 'easy' to read. Before they can make sense of them, children need to know that the pictures have to be read in a certain sequential order. The layout of the illustrations in some books can make it quite difficult to know where to start and some books also carry a dual narrative. These books require the reader to use complex skills in order for them to be interpreted correctly and very young children will need support with them. An example of such books are *The Angel and the Soldier Boy* and *Little Pickle*, both by Peter Collington, and Jan Ormerod's *Moonlight* and *Sunshine*.

The advantage of wordless picture books is that they do not require children to decode a written text and so all children can access them at one level or another and, of course, they have to speak in order to tell the story.

The opportunities for talk and discussion are many. You might consider asking children to think of what words would have been used had this been a written text. Ask them to consider what the illustrator uses instead of adjectives and how the pictures show verbs and indicate speech.

The following activity also uses images to inspire discussion and debate.

Activity 5 – Sequencing pictures to tell a narrative

Aims – Choose words with precision, organise what they say, listen to others' reactions, take turns in speaking, relate their contribution to what has gone before, take different views into account.

What to do – Divide the class into small groups of approximately three children. Place six to eight pictures in an envelope or plastic wallet that, when sequenced, tell a story, and give a pack to each group.

Tell the children that they are going to use the pictures to make up a story. Explain that to do this task they will have to co-operate with each other because they must all agree what order the pictures should go in and what the story might be.

Ask them to take two or three pictures from the top of the pack in the envelope. You will have to emphasise no cheating by peeking at the other pictures. When you place the pictures in the packs try to make sure that they are in a different order for each group. This is so that when the children lay out their images to order them they will not be influenced by what the other groups are doing. When the children have discussed the images and decided on an order, they should place the pictures in front of them.

Next ask them to take two more pictures from their pack. Ask the children to add them to their sequence. They need to discuss in their group where they should put the pictures in relationship to those they have already. Does this alter the narrative or order in any way? Now tell them to add the remaining pictures.

While the children are making their various sequences spend some time walking around the groups and listening to their discussions. Offer some support if you feel it is really needed but try to let them lead.

When all the pictures are sequenced compare work from different groups. Ask for some volunteers to say why they chose to sequence them as they did. What was the story behind the pictures? Did they all have the same order and were the ideas for their storylines the same? Did it matter in what order the pictures were sequenced?

Resources required – Any series of pictures that can be ordered sequentially.

Cross-curricular links – Literacy.

When to do it – In a literacy lesson during a lesson on narrative or story structure.

Use of teaching assistants – Help monitor the class, support a selected group, support the class alongside the teacher.

NLS and Foundation Stage objectives

Foundation Stage – Communication, language and literacy

Language for communication
Begin to use more complex sentences.

Use language for an increasing range of purposes.

Consistently develop a simple story, explanation or line of questioning.

Initiate conversation, attend to and take account of what others say, and use talk to resolve disagreement.

Respond to simple instructions.

Use a widening range of words to express or elaborate ideas.

Interact with others, negotiating plans and activities and taking turns in conversation.

Language for thinking
Talk activities through, reflecting on and modifying what they are doing.

Use talk to connect ideas, explain what is happening and anticipate what might happen next.

Use talk to organise, sequence and clarify thinking, ideas, feelings and events.

Reading
Re-tell narratives in the correct sequence, drawing on language patterns of stories.

Reception Year

Text level
T7 To use knowledge of familiar texts to re-enact or re-tell to others recounting the main points in correct sequence.

Year 1 Term 2

Text level
T4 To re-tell stories, giving the main points in sequence and to notice differences between written and spoken forms in re-telling, e.g. by comparing oral versions with the written text; to refer to relevant phrases and sentences.

T5 To identify and record some key features of story language from a range of stories, and to practise reading and using them, e.g. in oral re-tellings.

Year 1 Term 3

Text level
T5 To re-tell stories, to give the main points in sequence and to pick out significant incidents.

T6 To prepare and re-tell stories orally, identifying and using some of the more formal features of story language.

Year 2 Term 2

Text level

T7 To prepare and re-tell stories individually and through role-play in groups, using dialogue and narrative from text.

PNS objectives – Speaking, listening and learning

Year 1 Term 2

5. Speaking

To re-tell stories, ordering events using story language, e.g. using different techniques to recall and invent well-structured stories.

Link with NLS text objectives 4 and 5.

6. Listening

To listen and follow instructions accurately, asking for help and clarification if necessary, e.g. learning about the purpose of instructions, devising and following more complex instructions.

7. Group discussion and interaction

To take turns to speak, listen to others' suggestions and talk about what they are going to do, e.g. devising simple rules for turn-taking and contributing in groups.

Further comments and suggestions – Not only is this activity good for developing speaking and listening skills but it also helps raise awareness of the sequential nature of narrative. Talking through the story behind the pictures can help children develop an understanding of the importance of cohesion in a text. When working with very young children I have found that using no more than three or four images works best.

I have done this activity with the whole class but it can be done as a group activity if you feel that is more manageable.

An extension of this activity, when the children are reading to a certain level of fluency or with older children, is to cut up a written text into sections and get the children to sort them out and order them. They can then explain how they did it, problems encountered, how they overcame them, etc. This is also a good activity to help show the importance of text cohesion.

Other texts

Don't forget that non-fiction books also go down well and can really generate interest, involvement and discussion.

Other visual texts such as films and cartoon programmes from children's TV also make excellent stimulus for talk and discussion. The British Film Institute have produced a video of film shorts for Key Stages 1 and 2 that are also great to use in literacy and cross-curricular settings.

The activities described here are a selection of ones that I have used successfully and generally speaking they are easy to implement. Remember, whenever you read a book to children you are providing opportunities for speaking, listening and questioning while feeding their imaginations and furthering their learning.

Circle time and talk games

This chapter includes:

- Rules for circle time

- Some ideas for circle-time activities

- The effectiveness of puppets

- Talk games such as 'Chinese whispers' and 'Word tennis'.

Many of the activities in this book require children to work together co-operatively. We all know that in real life this can be a problem and have experienced the child who seems to cause disharmony whichever group they work with. Self-esteem can have a lot to do with how a child behaves and circle time can be a good way of tackling problems of low self-esteem.

I have included a few selected circle-time activities that I felt were successful, some of which helped raise self-esteem and all of which encouraged speaking and listening. I would suggest that anyone who wishes to find out about more about circle-time activities and the thinking behind the concept should read Jenny Mosley's book *Quality Circle Time* (1996).

I first encountered circle time in 1994 while working alongside a teacher in a Year 1 class. I try to do circle time as often as possible but this is not always as regular as I would like it to be. I usually try to fit it in towards the end of the week. Sometimes we focus on a light-hearted subject, or depending what has occurred during the week, something more thought-provoking. I have used impromptu circle times to try to resolve particular crises that have arisen, such as fights, name-calling or wanting mummies.

There are a few simple rules that apply to circle time that the children should be aware of before it happens. Each class may have their own slight variation but the basic principles should remain the same. These are as follows:

- Everyone, including adults present, sits in a circle. This can be on the floor or on chairs if the children are older.

- All present have an opportunity to speak but no one has to speak if they don't want to.

- Everyone must listen to the speaker.

- A small object is passed around the circle (a soft toy is ideal) and only the individual holding the object may speak.

- There must be no put-downs or making fun of individuals.

- Names of people are never mentioned unless it is to say something good about them.

- Everything said in circle time is confidential.

- By observing these rules children are been given an opportunity to express opinions in a secure environment, where they will be accepted and respected.

As mentioned, circle time is good for helping issues of self-esteem but for the purposes of this book I have concentrated on the benefits to speaking and listening.

Activity 1 – I feel proud because . . .

Aims – Speak with clear diction and appropriate intonation, choose words with precision, focus on the main point, take into account the needs of the listeners, sustain concentration, listen to others, take turns in speaking.

What to do – Seat the children in a circle facing inwards, with a chosen individual in the middle. Ask the children to pass a soft toy around the circle. As the toy is passed along, each child takes it in turns to say something positive about the child in the middle. This is one of the few occasions when I insist that each child must contribute.

Young children can sometimes find it hard to know where to start. I usually suggest a start to the sentence, which gives them a frame with which to continue, in this case 'I like Mitchell because . . .' or whatever the name of the child in the middle is. As the children make their comments, jot down each new comment on a piece of paper.

At the end of the session read back to the child what their friends have said about them and you will see them positively glow with pride. After this, write out the comments on a certificate to give to the child to take home; they will really treasure it. The wording on the certificates that I use read something like this: 'I feel proud because my friends said . . .' and then list the comments you wrote down during the session. This does not take very long and is well worth it. Remember to make a list of each child that has been in the middle in order that everyone is eventually included. This is an activity that is spread over the year.

Resources required – Soft toy, certificates.

Cross-curricular links – PSHE, RE.

When to do it – Whenever fits best into school timetable – a slot needs to be made available but this can vary from week to week. It can be done as an RE lesson, or to raise awareness of any pertinent issues in PSHE.

Use of teaching assistants – To make notes at the same time as the teacher in case something is missed, join in session with own contribution.

NLS and Foundation Stage objectives

Foundation Stage – Communication, language and literacy

Language for communication
Use language for an increasing range of purposes.

Sustain attentive listening, responding to what they have heard by relevant comments, questions or actions.

Respond to simple instructions.

Speak clearly and audibly with confidence and control and show awareness of the listener (for example, by use of conventions such as greetings, 'please' and 'thank you').

PNS objectives – Speaking, listening and learning

Year 1 Term 1

2. Listening
To listen with sustained concentration, e.g. identifying points of interest when listening to an explanation.

Year 3 Term 2

31. Group discussion and interaction
To actively include and respond to all members of the group, e.g. encouraging contributions by use of questions, eye contact and people's names when discussing an issue.

Further comments and suggestions – It can sometimes seem difficult to find a slot for one more extra thing but it is worth finding time for a regular circle-time session. I know of a teacher who used circle time every day in order to calm a particularly difficult situation in her class. Over time the situation improved greatly and although there were still problems they were nothing compared to those before the circle-time sessions began.

Don't forget to make sure you are part of the circle and add your own positive comments. I think positive comments coming from an adult are particularly appreciated.

The focus of the next activity is quite light-hearted and the same format can be used for a number of different focuses, which I mention in the further comments and suggestions.

Activity 2 – If I were a traditional story character I would be . . .

Aims – Speak with clear diction and appropriate intonation, choose words with precision focus on the main point, take into account the needs of the listeners, sustain concentration, listen to others, take turns in speaking, give reasons for opinions.

What to do – Seat the children in a circle as in the previous activity. Tell them to think of fairy and traditional story characters and decide who they would like to be. You may need to give them the starting point of their sentence by telling them to begin by saying, 'If I could be a traditional story character I would be . . .'. Pass the toy around the circle so that each child can have their say.

Resources required – Soft toy or object to pass around.

Cross-curricular links – Literacy, PSHE.

When to do it – At your usual circle-time slot, after literacy work on fairy stories or traditional stories.

Use of teaching assistants – To take part in the circle, help with class management.

NLS and Foundation Stage objectives

Foundation Stage – Communication, language and literacy

Language for communication
Use language for an increasing range of purposes.

Sustain attentive listening, responding to what they have heard by relevant comments, questions or actions.

Respond to simple instructions.

Speak clearly and audibly with confidence and control and show awareness of the listener (for example, by use of conventions such as greetings, 'please' and 'thank you').

PNS objectives – Speaking, listening and learning

Year 1 Term 1

2. Listening
To listen with sustained concentration, e.g. identifying points of interest when listening to an explanation.

Year 3 Term 2

31. Group discussion and interaction
To actively include and respond to all members of the group, e.g. encouraging contributions by use of questions, eye contact and people's names when discussing an issue.

Further comments and suggestions – An extension of this could be to ask the children to say why they made that choice. This can be quite hard for some children. Try to encourage the children to have their own ideas and not copy friends if possible.

Some other light-hearted focuses that work well using this format are: 'If I were a colour I would like to be . . .', 'If I were an animal I would like to be . . .', 'When I grow up I would like to be . . .'.

On a more serious note some of the focuses might be: 'I was scared when . . .', 'I don't like it when . . .', 'I feel nervous when . . .'.

Puppets

I had heard talk about puppets from various educational agencies, colleagues in other schools and educational publications but discovered the pulling power of a puppet for myself, quite by chance, about six years ago. I had a challenging class of streetwise Year 3s. Their behaviour and their ability to cope with each other and school would decline as the day progressed. It was always a struggle to get everyone settled onto the carpet after lunch, ready for register and the afternoon session.

One day, as the children came into the classroom after a particularly argumentative lunchtime, I picked up a glove puppet that had been left in my classroom from morning play. I popped it (a racoon, with a long, ringed tail) onto my hand, waggled it about and said, in a very bad American accent, something like this, 'Hey, little buddies, I'm gonna see who is first on the carpet and then I can say a real big howdy to them.' The effect was magic! Within seconds, 31 children were sitting on the carpet absolutely fixated with Ricky the Racoon. I was amazed at how the children responded to him. If someone had told me that this is what the children's reaction would have been, I do not think I would have believed them.

Since then I have used puppets in various ways and for various reasons in my classes, not all the time but always with the same delighted reaction from the children. A lot of the time it has not been an activity as such but more of an occasion, such as at year group gatherings and in assemblies.

The following activity uses a puppet and is also a circle-time activity. I have decided to use it here as an example of just how effective puppets can be in encouraging speaking, listening and concentration.

Before we go into the activity I need to explain about a large grey wolf arm puppet that I acquired from the Puppets by Post company. He has teeth that can be folded up or left down to make him fiercer but he was never fierce in my class. I introduced him to my Year 1 class as BB, short for 'Big Bad', but he never really took on that characteristic. The children all loved him straight away and because he is so realistic – most of them thought he was real.

I used BB with phonics games, and as a treat for them all being extra good and in a number of other ways. He became the leader of our Year 1 'wolf pack', the children all being his little 'wolfie' friends. They would try to behave well for him and he made a profound difference to the confidence in speaking of one small girl. This particular child would speak so quietly she could barely be heard. Her mother said she was very noisy at home so it seemed that in the school setting she did not feel comfortable or secure enough to speak audibly.

Activity 3 – A puppet in circle time – feeling good about yourself

Aims – Speak with clear diction and appropriate intonation, choose words with precision, organise what they say, focus on the main point, take into account the needs of the listeners, sustain concentration, listen to others, take turns in speaking.

What to do – Seat the children in an inward-facing circle, including yourself with your puppet. Explain that the puppet is feeling sad because he doesn't like something about himself. Tell them that they must cheer him up by showing him how to think of all the good things about himself by saying something positive about themselves. Pass the toy around and when it comes to the puppet let him say something he likes about himself.

Resources required – A puppet, a soft toy or object to pass around.

Cross-curricular links – PSHE, RE.

When to do it – As a PSHE or RE session on feelings, differences between people, being kind, etc., at your usual circle-time session.

Use of teaching assistants – To take part in the circle, help with class management.

NLS and Foundation Stage objectives
Foundation Stage – Communication, language and literacy

Language for communication
Use language for an increasing range of purposes.

Sustain attentive listening, responding to what they have heard by relevant comments, questions or actions.

Respond to simple instructions.

Use a widening range of words to express or elaborate ideas.

Speak clearly and audibly with confidence and control and show awareness of the listener (for example by use of conventions such as greetings, 'please' and 'thank you').

PNS objectives – Speaking, listening and learning
Year 1 Term 1

2. Listening
To listen with sustained concentration, e.g. identifying points of interest when listening to an explanation.

Year 3 Term 2

31. Group discussion and interaction
To actively include and respond to all members of the group, e.g. encouraging contributions by use of questions, eye contact and people's names when discussing an issue.

Further comments and suggestions – When I used this activity, I told the children that BB was sad because he didn't like his boring grey fur. He wanted to be colourful like a rainbow fish or striking like a zebra. They were horrified and not only said what they liked about themselves but also what they liked about BB too.

When it was the turn of my small quiet girl, I asked her to say something to BB to cheer him up but he would need to be able to hear her. She spoke in a voice loud enough for the whole class to hear without straining their ears. We all cheered. This of course was not the end to her quiet speaking but it was a great start. We all knew she could do it and the whole class encouraged and supported her to speak audibly from then on.

Finger puppets can be just as effective as their more elaborate cousins. I have used them effectively in maths and for other subjects.

I imagine that there are some of you who really do not think you would feel comfortable using a puppet. I can only urge you to give it a try. The children will not be focused on you, so however silly you think you appear they will not care. When you are working the puppet you can have him talk in your ear like Sooty and translate what he says to the children, or speak out loud like Ricky Racoon. Whatever you decide to do the children will love it. Give it a go!

Talk games

There are so many games that encourage speaking and listening and help concentration that it seems odd that all our children are not amazingly articulate, with the ability to listen and sustain concentration for hours. I have included a few here, some of which are party games that I played at my children's parties and can remember playing myself. They are fun but they are also invaluable in helping the development of speaking and listening.

Children will often say, after a speaking and listening session, 'We haven't done any work this morning, Miss.' I think that children should understand that speaking and listening are 'work' and they need to know why it is important, and how it helps them to learn.

Activity 4 – Chinese whispers

Aims – Speak clearly, listen carefully, sustain concentration.

What to do – Seat the children in an inward-facing circle. Start the game by whispering a phrase or sentence to a child. That child then passes on what they have heard by whispering to the next child, and so on all around the circle until it reaches the last one, who has to say out loud what they have heard. This is then compared to the original sentence.

Play the game again, choosing a child to say the beginning sentence.

Resources required – None.

Cross-curricular links – None specifically but phrases could be said around a particular subject or topic.

When to do it – In odd spare moments such as at the end of the day, before play or lunchtime. It will depend on your individual school's routine to some extent.

Use of teaching assistants – To support individuals, help monitor class behaviour.

NLS and Foundation Stage objectives

Foundation Stage – Communication, language and literacy

Language for communication
Use language for an increasing range of purposes.

Sustain attentive listening, responding to what they have heard by relevant comments, questions or actions.

Respond to simple instructions.

Further comments and suggestions – It usually transpires that the finishing sentence is nothing like the original one, much to the children's amusement.

Be aware that some children may not want to take part. Don't force the issue: let them be missed out if they are really unwilling. In time when they see it is good fun they usually come round and begin to join in. I have found that this game can take a bit of practice. One Year 1 class found it so difficult to play that the message never made it more than half-way around the circle. I left it for a while and then tried it again later and they were much better at it.

When I played this game as a child one of the rules was that the whisperer was not allowed to repeat the phrase. This meant that you had to listen extra carefully. You might find that the children find this quite difficult, in which case allow the phrase to be repeated.

The next activity is a party game that many of you will know. John Burningham's book *The Shopping Basket* uses the same idea as a basis for the narrative. As with all these games, people have their own slightly different versions. This is the one I used to play as a child and have used with my own class.

Activity 5 – I went to the shops and I bought . . .

Aims – Organise what they say, focus on the main points, sustain concentration, take turns in speaking, relate their contributions to what has gone before.

What to do – The children can sit either in a circle or as a class group. Explain that they are going to begin a sentence about one thing they bought from the shops, and someone else will repeat it and add another object. The first time you play it you can start them off: 'I went to the shops and I bought some carrots.' Choose a child and help them to repeat the sentence, with an addition: 'I went to the shops and I bought some carrots and apples' and then choose a different child to continue.

It does not matter what the children decide to 'buy' – the items can be as silly as they like, but they have to try to remember them in the correct order. This gets quite difficult as the list grows longer. Children can offer to continue the sentence or you can choose individuals to continue. Try to do this sensitively; choose those children who find it more difficult to begin the sentences.

This game is meant to be fun. Children should not be made to feel they have failed if they can't remember the list. As the class get better at it you can see if they can beat their own record.

Resources required – None.

Cross-curricular links – No specific links.

When to do it – At the end of the day before home time, any time when there are a few moments to fill.

Use of teaching assistants – To support individuals, give prompts, oversee class in general.

NLS and Foundation Stage objectives
Foundation Stage – Communication, language and literacy
Language for communication
Use language for an increasing range of purposes.

Sustain attentive listening, responding to what they have heard by relevant comments, questions or actions.

Respond to simple instructions.

Further comments and suggestions – A variation of this is to have all the items on the shopping list beginning with the same letter so that you get a long alliterative list.

These next activities are particularly good for developing listening skills. PE is an area of the curriculum that can provide some excellent opportunities for listening. These activities are both fun and are very good for seeing how hard it is for some children to listen and maintain concentration for a period of time.

This activity is particularly good with older children but I have played it successfully with Year 1s.

Activity 6 – Ladders

Aims – Enhance listening skills, sustain concentration, follow instructions.

What to do – Put the children into pairs and ask them to sit in two rows facing each other with their legs extended, flat on the floor and together with their feet touching. The effect of this should be that the children's legs resemble the rungs of a ladder. Make sure that there is a space of at least 30cm between the children. If you have quite a large class you can divide them into two groups, so that the rows are not so long.

Next give each pair of children a number starting at 1 and working down the row until the last pair. This applies even if you have two groups, and then you will have two pairs of number 1s and so on. Make sure that each pair knows which number they are by repeating it back to you. Now you are ready to begin.

It is a good idea to have a walk-through if the children have never played this before because it can be quite confusing, especially for younger children. You shout a number and that pair of children has to stand and run up the 'ladder' (the children's legs). When they get to the top of the ladder they split up, one to the left and the other right and run down each side of the ladder to the bottom and then back up the ladder to their places.

If you have two groups then the number applies to both groups. The child who gets back to their seat first is the winner. Be warned that this game is always really popular and can generate a lot of noise. If you want to make it more competitive you can have the rows as teams and keep a tally of how many children get back first in each row.

Resources – None.

Cross-curricular links – PE, PSHE.

When to do it – As part of a PE lesson.

Use of teaching assistants – To help organise the groups in the initial setting up, help decide which child gets back first, keep the tally, oversee the other group if there is more than one.

NLS and Foundation Stage objectives
Foundation Stage – Communication, language and literacy

Language for communication
Sustain attentive listening, responding to what they have heard by relevant comments, questions or actions.

Respond to simple instructions.

PNS objectives – Speaking, listening and learning

Year 1 Term 2

6. Listening

To listen and follow instructions accurately, asking for help and clarification if necessary, e.g. learning about the purpose of instructions, devising and following more complex instructions.

Further comments and suggestions – The children have to listen carefully to the instructions for this game and it can take some time before they really get the idea, especially which way to turn at the top of the ladder. Be patient.

They also have to listen very carefully for their number. As they become more familiar with the game, try calling two or even three numbers together! Not only do they need to respond to their number, but also they have to remember where their place in the row is.

Another activity that I have played with children in PE is also good fun and requires children to listen carefully before acting. It is very simple to set up and carry out.

Activity 7 – Crusts and crumbs

Aims – Enhance listening skills, sustain concentration, follow instructions.

What to do – Divide the class into two; I usually divide them into boys and girls as this adds a certain competitive dimension. Ask the boys to stand in a line along the wall at one side of the gym/hall facing the girls, who should stand along the opposite wall facing the boys.

Make a line at an equal distance from both boys and girls across the floor. You can do this by laying out skipping ropes or placing some cones or markers across the hall. You should now have two lines of children at either side of the hall, with a dividing line down the middle of the hall at equal distance from each set of children.

Next tell one line of children that they are 'crusts' and the other they are 'crumbs'. Make sure you remember which is which – it can get confusing! Explain to the children that you are going to shout out either 'crusts' or 'crumbs' and when they hear the one that refers to them they must all run to the line marked down the middle of the hall floor and back again. They can only run on their word; if they run and it is not their word they have to sit down for the rest of the game. This also applies if they are too slow at starting because they were not listening.

The winning group is the one who after a few goes have the most people still in it. Depending on time, you can play it until there are just a few individuals left in and they can be deemed the best listeners.

Resources required – None.

Cross-curricular links – PE, PSHE.

When to do it – As part of a PE lesson, at the end of a PE lesson, before the calming-down activity.

Use of teaching assistants – To help decide who is in or out, help with general class management.

NLS and Foundation Stage objectives

Foundation Stage – Communication, language and literacy

Language for communication
Sustain attentive listening, responding to what they have heard by relevant comments, questions or actions.

Respond to simple instructions.

PNS objectives – Speaking, listening and learning

Year 1 Term 2

6. Listening
To listen and follow instructions accurately, asking for help and clarification if necessary, e.g. learning about the purpose of instructions, devising and following more complex instructions.

Further comments and suggestions – This seems to be a very easy game but because both words begin with 'cru' the children must really listen for the whole word before they run. It is surprising how 'crusts' will start to run when it should be 'crumbs' and vice versa. The children must also listen for themselves and not copy the rest because the others might have got it wrong.

I have found that children love to play this over and over again – you will be fed up with it before they are! You can make it more fun by occasionally shouting for both crusts and crumbs to run together.

As with many of these games, not only are they good for listening skills but they are also good for developing social skills.

This next game is good for both speaking and listening skills. A similar activity is described in the PNS Speaking, listening and learning pack as 'Word tennis'. I know it from party games as 'When suddenly . . .', which is the title I shall give it here.

Activity 8 – When suddenly . . .

Aims – Speak with clear diction and appropriate intonation, choose words with precision, organise what they say, take into account the needs of their listeners, sustain concentration, take turns in speaking, relate their contribution to what has gone before.

What to do – This activity can be played in partners or groups. Explain that they are all going to take part in telling a story. Someone will start the story off, e.g. 'In an old house, high on a hill there lived . . .', and then the next person continues the story from where the other left off.

The best way for children to get the idea is for you to model it. You can do this by using other adults in the room or if there are none, by using selected articulate children to help.

After the session you might like some of the groups or pairs to demonstrate their work.

Resources required – None.

Cross-curricular links – Literacy.

When to do it – Within a unit of work in literacy on narrative, in any spare minutes of the day such as before home time, lunch, etc.

Use of teaching assistants – To help model the activity, to work with selected pairs or groups or to patrol the class as the teacher focuses on selected children, support individuals to enable them to be part of the story.

NLS and Foundation Stage objectives

Foundation Stage – Communication, language and literacy

Language for communication
Use intonation, rhythm and phrasing to make their meaning clear to others.

Begin to use more complex sentences.

Use language for an increasing range of purposes.

Sustain attentive listening, responding to what they have heard by relevant comments, questions or actions.

PNS objectives – Speaking, listening and learning

Year 1 Term 1

2. Listening
To listen with sustained concentration, e.g. identifying points of interest when listening to an explanation.

5. Speaking
To re-tell stories, ordering events using story language, e.g. using different techniques to recall and invent well-structured stories.

Link with NLS text objectives 4 and 5.

Year 2 Term 2

17. Speaking
To tell real and imagined stories using the conventions of familiar story language, e.g. including relevant detail, keeping the listeners' interest and sustaining an account.

Link with NLS text objective 7.

Further comments and suggestions – The game I know as 'When suddenly . . .' is so called because each part of the story finishes with the phrase 'when suddenly', e.g. 'One day a small boy was walking down the road when suddenly . . .', and the next person picks up the narrative: '. . . a large wolf leapt out of the bushes, growling fiercely. The little boy turned to run away when suddenly . . .'.

The ideas are very similar; you could try doing both. Word tennis can also be played with each child only saying one word each time to continue the story.

Be aware that some children may find this activity extremely challenging. This does not mean that they should be not be included but rather that they are offered support in a discreet way to enable them to make their contribution and feel valued.

References and book list

References

Department for Education and Skills (1998) *The National Literacy Strategy – Framework for Teaching*. London: DfES.

Department for Education and Skills (1999a) *Progression in Phonics*. London: DfES.

Department for Education and Skills (1999b) *Playing with Sounds* (a supplement to *Progression in Phonics*). London: DfES.

Department for Education and Skills/Qualifications and Curriculum Authority (2003) *Speaking, Listening, Learning: Working with Children in Key Stages 1 and 2*. London: DfES.

DfES/QCA (2000) *The National Curriculum – Handbook for Primary Teachers in England*. London: DfES.

Qualifications and Curriculum Authority (1999) *Guidance for Teaching Speaking and Listening Skills in Key Stages 1 and 2*. London: QCA.

Spotlight on Poetry (1999) *Classic Poems 1* (collected by Brian Moses and David Orme). London: Collins Educational.

Book list

Poetry and rhyme

Colin McNaughton (1987) *There's An Awful Lot Of Weirdos In Our Neighbourhood*. London: Walker Books.

Zita Necome (1990) *Ten in the Bed (and other counting rhymes)*. London: Walker Books.

The Works (2000) (poems chosen by Paul Cookson). London: Macmillan Children's Books.

This Little Puffin (1969) (compiled by Elizabeth Matterson). London: Penguin Books.

Kaye Umansky and Nick Sharratt (1999) *Tickle My Nose*. London: Puffin Books

Kaye Umansky and Nick Sharratt (2002) *Wiggle My Toes*. London: Puffin Books.

Picture books

Anthony Browne (1995) *Gorilla*. London: Walker Books.

Anthony Browne (1997) *The Tunnel*. London: Walker Books.

Anthony Browne (2000) *Willy the Dreamer*. London: Walker Books.

Anthony Browne (2002) *Changes*. New York: Farrar, Straus and Giroux.

John Burningham (1992) *The Shopping Basket*. London: Red Fox.

Lauren Child (2000a) *Beware of the Storybook Wolves*. London: Hodder Children's Books.

Lauren Child (2000b) *I Will Not Ever Never Eat a Tomato*. London: Orchard Books.

Lauren Child (2001) *I am Not Sleepy and Will Not Go to Bed*. London: Orchard Books.

Lauren Child (2003) *I am Too Absolutely Small for School*. London: Orchard Books.

Helen Cooper (1998a) *Pumpkin Soup*. London: Doubleday.

Helen Cooper (1998b) *The House Cat*. London: Scholastic.

Sarah Dyer (2001) *Five Little Fiends*. London: Bloomsbury Children's Books.

Nigel Gray (1998) *I'll Take you to Mrs Cole* (illustrated by Michael Foreman). London: Andersen.

Sally Grindley and Peter Utton (1999) *Shhh*. London: Hodder Children's Books.

Shirley Hughes (1994) *The Big Alfie Out of Doors Storybook*. London: Red Fox.

Shirley Hughes (1998) *The Big Alfie and Annie Rose Storybook*. London: The Bodley Head.

Pat Hutchins (2001) *Rosie's Walk*. London: Red Fox.

Satoshi Kitamura (1999) *Me and My Cat*. London: Red Fox.

Satoshi Kitamura (2003) *Lily Takes a Walk*. Bradfield: Happy Cat Books.

David Lloyd (2000) *Polly Molly Woof Woof* (illustrated by Charlotte Hard). London: Walker Books.

Michael Rosen (1993) *We're Going on a Bear Hunt* (illustrated by Helen Oxenbury). London: Walker Books.

Chris Van Allsburg (1985) *The Mysteries of Harris Burdick*. London: Andersen.

Barbara Walker (1977) *Teeny-Tiny and the Witch-Woman* (illustrated by Michael Foreman). London: Andersen.

Chris Wormell (2003) *George and the Dragon*. London: Red Fox.

Wordless picture books

Jeannie Baker (2002) *Window*. London: Walker Books.

Quentin Blake (1995) *Clown*. London: Red Fox.

Peter Collington (1986) *Little Pickle*. London: Methuen Children's Books.

Peter Collington (1987) *The Angel and the Soldier Boy*. London: Methuen Children's Books.

Philippe Dupasquier (1992) *I Can't Sleep*. London: Andersen.

Shirley Hughes (1991) *Up and Up*. London: Red Fox.

Jan Ormerod (2004a) *Sunshine*. London: Frances Lincoln.

Jan Ormerod (2004b) *Moonlight*. London: Frances Lincoln.

John Prater (1996) *The Gift* (new edition). London: Random House Children's Books.

General interest

Bfi Education *Starting Stories* – www.bfi.org.uk
Jenny Mosley (1996) *Quality Circle Time*. Wisbech: LDA.
National Gallery *Take One Picture* – www.takeonepicture.org.uk
Puppets by Post – www.puppetsbypost.com

Index

action songs 14
alliteration 11–14
areas for talk 24–5
artefacts 25–6

bags, talk 61–5
books 91–2
    see also picture books

cartoon programmes 91
castle making 19–21
characters
    historical 36–7
    improvisation 38–40
    story 30–2
'Chinese whispers' 99–100
circle time 93–4
    activities 94–7
    and puppets 98–9
conscious alley 72
corners
    home 22–4
    talk 28–9
'Crusts and crumbs' 103–4
curriculum
    questions 71–2
    and talk 24–5

debates 72–5
    building proposal 75–7
description of paintings 84–5

drawing of paintings 84–5

expressive reading/recitation 8–11

fairy story characters 30–2
film programmes 91–2
freeze-frames 81–3

games 14
    talk 99–106
'Goldilocks and the bears' house' 73–5
'Guess the picture' 79–81
'Guess the traditional or fairy storey
        character' 30–2

historical characters 36–7
home corners 22–4
hot-seating 32–7

'I feel proud because . . .' 94–5
'I went to the shops and I bought . . .' 101
'If I were a traditional story character . . . '
        96–7
improvisation, paired 38–40
investigation 25–8

'Ladders' 102–3

'Make a castle' 19–21
'Make a home corner' 22–4
'Make a shop' 16–18

materials 26–8
mime
    class involvement 43–6
    introductory activities 40–3

narrative, picture sequencing 89–91
news sharing 66–8
non-fiction books 91

objects/artefacts 25–6
open questions 71–2
oral story retelling 56–61
oral work 13–14

paintings 78–81
    freeze-frames 81–3
    visualisation/drawing 84–5
paired improvisation 38–40
picture books 85–8
    wordless 88
pictures 78
    'Guess the picture' 79–81
    sequencing 89–91
'Playing with alliteration' 11–14
poetry 3
puppets 97–9

questions 66–71
    across the curriculum 71–2

reading/recitation 8–11
rhymes 1–3
    silly 5–8
role-play areas 15–19

'Secret mimes' 41–3
self-confidence 30
sequencing of pictures 89–91
'Share a rhyme or song' 1–2
'Share a story bag' 48–52
'Share your news' 66–8
shop making 16–17
shops, debate 75–7

'Should Goldilocks have gone into the
    bears' house'? 73–5
'Should a take-away be built at the local
    shops?' 75–7
'Show and tell' 66–8
'Silly rhymes' 5–8
songs 1–3
    action 14
'Sorting syllables' 3–5
story
    bags 47–52
    boxes 61–5
    characters 30–2, 96–7
    retelling 53–5
        written and oral 56–61
    telling 52
syllables, sorting 3–5

talk
    about materials 26–8
    about objects/artefacts 25–6
    about picture book 86–8
    areas 24–5
    bags/tins 61–5
    corners 28–9
    and curriculum 24–5
    games 99–106
    and investigation 25–8
'Three Billy-Goats Gruff, The' 43–4
tins, talk 61–5
traditional story characters 30–2, 96–7
Twenty questions 69–70

visualisation of paintings 84–5

'We're Going on a Bear Hunt' 45–6
'What did one character say to the other?'
    38–40
'What's my number?' 70–1
'When suddenly . . .' 104–6
wordless picture books 88
written story retelling 56–61